# DISTRICT TARTAN AREAS

D0503214

England

Berwick-upon-Tweed

Tweed

Dunbar

St. Andrews
FIFE

Firth of Forth

Gala Water

ROXBURGH

Musselburgh

EDINBURGH

TWEEDSIDE

Ettrick

Ettrick

Strathearn

STIRLING AND
BANNOCKBURN

Cumbernauld

Moffat

Dunblane

Blairlogie
Menteith

Lennox

GLASGOW

Clyde

Nithsdale

Nith

STRATHCLYDE

East
Kilbride

PAISLEY

Eglinton

Largs

AYRSHIRE

CARRICK

Glen Trool
GALLOWAY

Rothesay

ARRAN

Firth of Clyde

Firth of Lorn

ARGYLL

Irish Sea

Isle of Man

ULSTER

© Shepheard – Walwyn (Publishers) Ltd.

# DISTRICT TARTANS

# DISTRICT TARTANS

By

## GORDON TEALL OF TEALLACH
### and
## PHILIP D. SMITH JR

Shepheard-Walwyn (Publishers) Ltd

First published in 1992 by
Shepheard-Walwyn (Publishers) Ltd
26 Charing Cross Road (Suite 34)
London WC2H 0DH

*British Library Cataloguing in Publication Data*
Teall, Gordon
     District tartans.
     1. Scotland. Tartans
     I. Title    II. Smith, Philip D.
     929'.9

     ISBN 0-85683-085-2

Typesetting by Alacrity Phototypesetters
Banwell Castle, Weston-super-Mare, Avon
Printed in Spain by Artes Graficas, Toledo
D.L.TO:1458-1992

# CONTENTS

**MAPS OF SCOTLAND**
District Tartan Areas            Front Endpaper
Former Countries and Modern Regions     Rear Endpaper

*Preface*     ix
*Introduction*     1

**SECTION I**
The Origin of District Tartans     5
District Tartans of Today     10
'Royal' District Tartans     14
Availability of District Tartans     16
Thread Counts     17
Colour Abbreviations     19

**SECTION II**
DISTRICT TARTANS OF SCOTLAND     21

**SECTION III**
DISTRICT TARTANS OF THE BRITISH ISLES
    OUTWITH SCOTLAND     135

**SECTION IV**
OTHER DISTRICT TARTANS     177

**APPENDICES**
1   Which Tartan Should I Wear?     247
2   The Law of Scotland Concerning Tartans     250
3   The Court of the Lord Lyon With Regard to Tartans     252
4   The Scottish Tartans Society     254
5   The Scottish Tartans Museum Trust     257
6   The Register of All Publicly Known Tartans     258
7   Glossary     260

*Index*     262

# ACKNOWLEDGEMENTS

The authors wish to acknowledge the encouragement, support and assistance of the many colleagues who have helped the concept of a book on district tartan to reach fruition. They are too numerous to mention individually, but we would particularly like to thank the members and staff of the Scottish Tartans Society and The Lord Lyon King of Arms and his assistants.

We are indebted to the many designers and tartan historians who have supplied details on particular setts. We also wish to thank the weavers whose work is illustrated here and the photographers for the care they have taken. The continued exhortation and encouragement of tartan enthusiasts throughout the world has helped to keep us on course.

GORDON TEALL OF TEALLACH
PHILIP D. SMITH, JR

# PREFACE

Tartan is evocative. Though some may be indifferent to its fascination, in others it is capable of arousing varying kinds and degrees of emotion: love, hostility, fear, joy, according to the beliefs and upbringing of the individual concerned. For many, it is a symbol of so much that they cherish: love for their families; affection for their clan or district; pride in their regiment; loyalty to their companies or associations. To the Germans of the First World War, the tartan-clad Highland regiments inspired fear, mingled with both hatred and respect for some of their most formidable opponents were the kilted warriors.

Today, for a few, tartan arouses hostility of another sort, even derision. Some Scots decry the tartan image of their country since they feel it impedes a proper appreciation of the technological achievements of modern Scotland. Wiser counsel, however, generally prevails, since tradition and modernity need not conflict but can complement one another. Indeed, a noteworthy development of the present day is the increasing number of major companies which are making use of specially designed commemorative tartans to emphasise their corporate identity. Joy, however, is one of the principal emotions associated with tartan. It is to those who find pleasure in understanding the significance of tartan that this book is dedicated.

It cannot be denied that very many people when asked, associate tartan with clans, especially the more well known ones, such as the MacDonalds, Campbells or MacLeans. Many books have been published illustrating clan tartans, giving comprehensive pedigrees of the families concerned. Only certain Scottish family names, however, have tartans specifically associated with them. Readers desirous of wearing tartan who can find no connection with such a family will find this book of special interest. They may have the choice of wearing a district tartan appropriate to the place of their origin, their residence, or a particular district or town with which they wish to identify as a sign of affection.

There has not been, until now, a publication which gives a comprehensive account of the district tartans. The authors of *District Tartans* have chosen fifty-six district tartans in Scotland

ix

which are linked by name with land: loosely defined areas without precise borders (e.g. Lochaber), Regions (e.g. Strathclyde), cities (e.g. Glasgow), towns (e.g. Stirling), villages (e.g. Blairlogie). Outwith Scotland, they have selected twenty relating to other divisions of the British isles, including the Republic of Ireland and a further thirty-four from the overseas countries of the British Commonwealth, the United States of America and the Netherlands. The authors, of course, are fully aware that controversy attends any discussion on district tartans. The same, however, can be said of clan tartans. It is all too easy to forget that the tartan associated with a particular personal name may have a history only one tenth as long as that of the family to which it relates. The authors and the Scottish Tartans Society make available to the public this first-ever illustrated reference book of Scottish 'district' tartans in the hope that these will receive more recognition and more display. *District Tartans* seeks to set out the facts with regard to each sett. It does not seek to delude the readers as some earlier authors did, neither does it pour scorn on those who endeavour to spread the use of tartan. The reader is left to make his own judgement.

GORDON TEALL OF TEALLACH
PHILIP D. SMITH JR

# INTRODUCTION

Tartan, is an art form — emotive and subjective. It has even been described as a three dimensional sculpture in wool. The authors of this book are conscious that this work might lead some of their readers to think of tartan more as a science than an art. Just as folksongs, once written down, lose the essence of their original spontaneity, so too does the recording of tartans change the artistic character of setts as they were woven before the Act of Proscription of 1746. This Act forbade the wearing of the 'Plaid, Philibeg, or little Kilt, Trowse, Shoulder Belts, or any Part whatsoever of what peculiarly belongs to the Highland garb'. When it was repealed in 1782, there was a great upsurge of interest in tartan but, by now, there was a desire to give setts specific names, particularly those of clans, though some were named after districts.

Few samples of tartan woven before the great revival of the late eighteenth century survive, though some setts were captured in portraiture. In those days, the yarns used for warp and weft were often different in texture, the former, for obvious reasons, being stronger. Shades of colours, too, changed with various dye batches of wool. Often, the sett varied also in warp and weft so that the resulting tartan looked greatly different from the symmetrical patterns so familiar today. Moreover, even after the thread counts had begun to be regularised during the early nineteenth century, the proportions often varied from sample to sample.

Since the end of the eighteenth century, the need to have a symbol of identity in the form of a tartan sett has steadily evolved. As a consequence thread counts for each particular pattern have become standardised. Few nowadays would dispute the wisdom of this. The same cannot be said for colour, however. Here the scope for individual preference remains. The idea of standardised colours by means of the international colour code has been mooted, but rejected by the leaders of the world of tartan. There are two reasons for this; the first is that standardised colours would limit the freedom of the weaver to blend the shades as he thinks fit. The other is the very practical reason that even with modern technology it is not easy to match

1

colours from yarn to yarn, or dye batch to dye batch. For both commercial and aesthetic reasons, however, the colours used for tartans today fall into three broad categories, ancient, modern and reproduction. These give the individual a choice of shade.

### Ancient colours

The use of the term 'ancient' confuses many uninitiated in tartan terminology. It has nothing at all to do with the year in which a tartan was first recorded. The shades used are of softish hues and represent the kind of colours obtained by the hand-dyes of yesterday when tartans were woven on home-looms. Originally most of these colours were obtained from plants although some were made of animal matter and minerals. Nowadays, there is little use made of natural dyes except by specialists, the ancient colours of today being synthetic dyes.

### Modern colours

During the nineteenth century, aniline dyes began to replace the older natural dyes previously used. Because of their new-ness, they came to be known as modern dyes. Generally 'modern' colours have harsher and more strident tones than the ancient.

### Reproduction colours

The concept of reproduction colours was introduced by D. C. Dalgleish Limited in 1946. The idea was to recreate the appear-ance of an old piece of tartan cloth found buried on Culloden moor in which the colours had faded due to ageing and staining by peat. The colours so obtained appeal to many because of the soft muted effect. The idea has been taken up by other firms of weavers, some of which use the terminologies 'muted, faded or weathered' to describe the same or a similar effect. There is perhaps a growing need to be more specific in this respect. 'Muted' might be used for those softer shades which give the impression of being slightly faded ancient colours. 'Weath-ered', which has more appealing implications than 'Repro-duction', might be better reserved for those tartans in which the simulated weathering of the colours is more pronounced, with a change of green to brown, for example.

Most manufacturers today try to standardise the colours of their own tartans in each category as far as is practical.

Colours, however, may vary from mill to mill. Indeed, the same sett can be seen in such differing tones that uninitiated observers might be forgiven for believing that they were looking at different tartans. Consequently, when orders are given for a particular tartan to be especially woven, it is wise to agree beforehand with the mill the colours to be used. Manufacturers will usually supply samples of yarn for this purpose.

Because of the increasing number of tartans, there is little room nowadays for a variation of the proportion of colours in a particular named tartan, as occurred frequently in the nineteenth century. Shades of colour, however, are a different matter. The newly designed tartans which are placed before the Council of the Scottish Tartans Society for formal accreditation vary greatly in their aesthetic appearance. Though all are technically correct, their visual impact upon person to person inspires a wide spectrum of response; proof enough that tartan, though now woven with scientific precision, is still an emotive art form.

# SECTION I

## THE ORIGIN OF
## DISTRICT TARTANS

District tartans have existed alongside clan and family tartan
for centuries. Stewart of Garth wrote of the early Highlanders:

> In dying and arranging the various colours of their tartans they displayed
> no small art and taste. Preserving at the same time the distinctive patterns
> (or setts as they were called) of the different clans, tribes, families and
> districts. Thus a MacDonald, a Campbell, a MacKenzie, etc. was known
> by his plaid; and in like manner the Athole, Glenorchy and other colours
> of different districts were easily distinguishable.[1]

District tartans were included on the earliest known lists of
manufactured tartans, those of William Wilson and Sons of
Bannockburn. The Wilsons were weaving and selling tartan in
the Highlands even prior to the repeal of the Act of Proscription and continued to be a major supplier of tartan for well over
a century. Their carefully preserved records give us invaluable
insights into the history of tartan.

Some tartans first recorded as 'district' have been identified
with a particular clan — the *breacan glas* of Badenoch is now the
'Hunting MacPherson', illustrative of the firm identification of
territory with clan. A few patterns are still both 'district' and
'clan'. The 'Argyll' was so identified by the Wilsons several
decades before the same pattern in lighter colours was published as the 'Campbell of Cawdor'.

The exact origin of tartan in Scotland is, however, simply
unknown despite several centuries of research and a large
amount of conjecture. The crossing of colour stripes in regular
patterns by the weaver is not unique to Scotland nor is the style
of weaving. In many folk cultures one finds the identification of
tribe, clan or locale by unique patterns of stripes and colours on
the body, on clothing or on accessories.

Tartan has been worn by the Highland Scots at least as far back
as the sixteenth century, perhaps replacing older less colourful
material. This 'quaint' costume was consistently mentioned by

travellers who saw the Highlanders at home and by those who saw Scottish mercenary soldiers abroad. In the seventeenth century the Highland Scot, living in a mountainous wilderness and speaking the 'Irish' language, were as picturesque and savage to other Europeans — including southern Scots and the English — as were the Lapps or the Albanians. A present-day comparison might be that of warring tribes of Afghanistan. At that time travel in the north of Scotland was exceedingly difficult. There were almost no roads suitable for wheeled traffic north of Edinburgh. Conditions almost guaranteed that people who lived together in small communities in the fertile shelter of the glens, isolated from other groups by water, mountains and barren moors, would be biologically related and sociologically cohesive. Identification was with place and people — and if transported from the place then kinship was with the people wherever they might be found.

In such a culture, tartan and the belted plaid were described by early writers as distinctively Highland. Martin Martin, a Gaelic-speaking Highlander whose work took him to the Outer Hebrides, wrote about 1695 in one of the first books on the region:

> Every Isle differs from each other in their fancy of making Plads as to the stripes in breadth and colours. The humour is as different through the mainland of the Highlands, in so far that they who have seen those places are able at first view of the man's Plad, to guess the place of his residence.

There has been much discussion about Martin's use of the word 'guess' in the passage quoted above. Some maintain that 'guess' implies a real uncertainty about the accuracy of the decision — that an observer could not at all be certain of the tartan wearer's place of residence. Others understand that the word 'guess' was narrower in definition in the seventeenth century. Although one could not preclude the possibility of error through lack of knowledge or the use of hand-me-down clothing, the word 'guess' was surely intended to be synonymous with 'identify with some reliability'. This seems more plausible, else Martin would not have bothered to make the point at all. He certainly intended his readers to know that a knowledgeable observer could look at a man's clothing and with reasonable accuracy identify his place of origin.

Martin was very specific that it was the *place* of residence that was apparent to the knowledgeable observer, not the Highlander's family. Secondly, Martin was careful to point out that this custom was found on both the Isles and the Mainland. Highlands in this general sense, of course, covered a much larger area than that administered by the present day Highland Regional Council. One of the earliest tartans recorded is that of the Countess of Lennox, whose name was derived from an area not far from modern Glasgow (see p. 90).

It is reasonable to believe that persons who lived in the same areas used the product of the same weavers who in turn employed local dyes and preferences in their cloth. Traces of this may still be seen today in that the majority of older clan tartans from the west of Scotland are in blue, black and green — MacLeod, MacNeil, MacDonald, Campbell and the 'Mull' tartan. A number of clans in the northeast use variations of the same pattern of blue or black and green stripes on a red ground — Macintosh, Robertson, MacGillivary, Grant, Murray. It is a mistake, however, as some recent researchers outwith Scotland have done, to attribute some hidden meaning, or ancient script, to the number, width or colour of stripes in particular setts. In most cases such details would have initially signified the personal preference of a particular weaver, or possibly those of his customer. More prosaically, the proportion of colours might have been influenced by the amount of any particular yarn immediately available to the weaver.

By the early 1700s the wearing of tartan had spread south, perhaps spurred by the rising sentiment of Scottish nationalism and the Jacobite cause. Contemporary portraits of many Lowland figures show them wearing tartan. Tartan was coming to be regarded as part of the Scottish national dress although the kilt itself at first remained the costume of the Highlander. Trousers, worn in both Highland and Lowland, were sometimes tartan. It is at this time that references to tartan became more numerous, including spasmodic association with place or clan.

The identification of tartan with vassalage or tenantry is supported by the earliest known references to a 'uniform clan' tartan, that of the Grants in 1703. Captain Hamilton of the Inverness garrison reported to his superior, General Maitland, on 23 July 1703, that '... the Laird of Grant ... has ordered 600 of his men in arms, in good order, with Tartane Coates all of one colour and fashion'. The uniform 'one colour and fashion' is specifically mentioned in the papers of the Grant family for the following year. On 27 July 1704, Alexander Grant of Grant, ordered all male tenants to have red and green tartan clothing and 'gun sword pistoll and durk' ready to assemble on forty-eight hours notice by the 8th of August.

James H. Grant, in his privately printed *Historical Notes on some Tartans Associated with the Clan Grant* (1985), points out that the order for each man to have 'Heighland Coates trewes and short hose of tartane red and Grein sett broad springed' does not necessarily imply that the patterns of each man were identical but only similar. He also points out that such an order coming only two weeks in advance of the dates established for a rendezvous indicates that the man probably already had the uniform coloured clothing on hand.

Of perhaps more interest to the student of both 'clan' and 'district' tartans is an earlier order of the Laird of Grant to his tenants in upper Strathspey, territory usually associated with the Clan MacPherson. On 20 July 1704, the Laird of Grant directed that 'Ronald Makdonald of Gelloway and Archbold Makdonald' tenants in Laggan in Badenoch were to be equipped with the 'red and Grein sett'. Here is a perfect example of tartan uniformity associated with land and tenantry rather than by name — MacDonalds who were tenants of the Laird of Grant were ordered to be outfitted in the same tartan type as all other Grant tenants. The Young Laird of Grant had seen military service on the continent and it is believed that he treated his male followers much as if they were regular soldiers. They were, after all, fencible men, ready to defend the Grant lands and interests — a uniformly equipped militia force of regimental strength which commanded the attention of the regular forces placed in the Highlands to keep the peace.

Wearing the colours chosen by the feudal lord, his livery, continued into the twentieth century. The adoption of a uniform tartan for followers of a Highland chief is the same custom. Later the tartan wearing would be extended to 'family' with dependents and descendents of the tenants accounting for many of the so-called 'septs', names associated with clans and families. A new settler on the lands of the chief would be expected to serve the new landlord in the same way as prior tenants. Tartan for many was undoubtedly associated with service rather than with blood.

James, Laird of Grant in the last quarter of the eighteenth century, wrote that he was trying to ascertain the exact pattern of the old 'Strathspey tartan' worn two generations earlier. This indicates that the chief himself associated the tartan with the region rather than the name of Grant. In the 1800s, Struan Robertson wore the 'Atholl tartan' before its adoption by the Murrays as a family sett and the adoption of the red and green 'Robertson' tartan.

The district tartan concept is truly old and probably more supported from a documented historical viewpoint than is the clan tartan. Even to this day there is a strong sense of place among Gaelic-speaking Highlanders; they will talk of 'a Barra man', 'a Lochaber man'. Identity with place is clear in the Gaelic greeting, *Failte do'n Duthaich* — Welcome to the country.

**Note**

1   David Stewart of Garth *Sketches of the Highlanders of Scotland* Vol 1, 1822, p. 79.

# DISTRICT TARTANS OF TODAY

District tartans in the British Isles are no longer confined to Scotland alone. They are to be found also in other areas which have a strong Celtic tradition. The pride of the Celtic race remains wherever one of the Celtic languages is still used as an everyday means of communication, or was so until comparatively recently.

Welsh, one branch of the Brythonic group of Celtic languages, is spoken by about a fifth of the population of Wales, which at the time of the 1981 census, was approaching three million. A second Brythonic tongue, Cornish, which has not been generally spoken in Cornwall since the late eighteenth century, is today used on a limited basis by enthusiasts who wish to encourage its preservation.

Branches of the Goidelic group of Celtic languages have survived in Ireland (particularly in the southwest), in the Isle of Man, and in Scotland, especially in the Hebrides. Irish and Scottish Gaelic are still the mother tongue of a relatively small minority of the respective populations of Ireland and Scotland. Manx is no longer in everyday use, though it still forms part of official parliamentary proceedings in the Isle of Man (which is self-governing). Like Cornish, Manx is spoken by groups of patriots, not all of whom were born on Mann, and it is taught in some of the local schools.

The Celtic languages, as a symbol of 'nationhood' in Cornwall, Wales, Ireland, Isle of Man and Scotland, are struggling hard to survive the onward tide of English, now an international language. The pride of separate identity has been epitomised in Scotland by tartan for hundreds of years. In the remainder of the lands of Celtic tradition, the development of tartans has taken place in the main since the Second World War. The phenomenon may be regarded as a desire, by some, though relatively few of their inhabitants, to emphasise the 'nationhood' of their countries by means other than by one of the Celtic languages.

Today, Cornish, Irish, Manx and Welsh tartans, like those of Scotland itself, are worn with pride not only by those families of Celtic descent but also those of Viking and Saxon origin.

Racial divisions, by blood alone, have become more blurred than surnames alone indicate, since from earliest times much intermarriage has taken place. National pride is often more a matter of geographical boundaries than racial origins.

It is all too easy, however, to idealise the reasons for the growth of tartan in the British Isles outwith Scotland and in consequence to overstate the case. In Ireland, for example, there are only three district tartans, Ulster, Clodagh and Tara. The kilt, which is not extensively worn, is usually made of green or saffron material. Tartan cloth, however, was used when making some late sixteenth and early seventeenth century garments worn in Ireland, although it may have been imported from Scotland. The discovery of wearing apparel of this period in a bog at Flanders near Dungiven, County Londonderry, Northern Ireland, in 1956 led to the introduction of the Ulster district tartan. The origin of the Clodagh tartan is similar, but is not so well documented being based upon a specimen reputed to have been found in the Bog of Allen in Southern Ireland. Like the Tara district tartan, the sett is derived from the Royal Stewart. Its ancestry, therefore, is possibly that it once belonged to a Scottish soldier, rather than to a native of the district. It is this uncertainty concerning the origin of Irish tartans, that would give substance to the view held by some of the leaders or organisations associated with the preservation of Ireland's heritage that tartans are not part of the native culture. This belief might help to explain why district tartans have not proliferated in Ireland to the same extent, for example, as they have in the Isle of Man.

In Wales, however, the position was somewhat different. Here, the Welsh Celtic Society, situated in Cardiff, was formed after the Second World War. The Society, was not only dedicated to preserving the Welsh language, but also wanted a dress that would associate the Welsh with other Celtic races. The tartan is an illustration of the tendency which has developed in post war years of choosing colours as symbols, namely those of the Welsh flag.

Another form of symbolism is illustrated in the Manx National tartan. On the Isle of Man, there was also a desire to be associated culturally with the other Celtic races and this led to the design of a tartan of which the colours represented the physical characteristics of the island. The same may be said for Cornwall, where again there has been an upsurge of interest in the county's Celtic past. The growing popularity of tartans in Cornwall has led to its neighbour Devon producing tartans symbolic in the choice of colours. More recently, Somerset tartans have been introduced.

Apart from those of Cornwall, Devon and Somerset, district tartans have not yet become established in England, on a large scale. Tweedside, however, is applicable to both sides of the Border. 'Berwick' was designed by a schoolgirl of the town in a competition run by Berwick Town Council. 'Durham' is an English tartan from the last century and appears amongst the records of William Wilson & Sons of Bannockburn during the second quarter of the nineteenth century. Although it was Wilsons' practice to give names of towns and districts to some of their patterns, this is the only non-Scottish town in their collection. Why the name occurs will probably never be known. Possibly, it was first sold to someone of that name, or to a resident of the city. In regard to England, there is a possibility that district tartans may evolve in the future, particularly in the North, in the areas roughly designated by the borders of the ancient Kingdom of Strathclyde.

Outwith the British Isles, the country which has given rise to most new district tartans has been Canada. Indeed, Nova Scotia was marginally ahead of the Isle of Man in producing its own district tartan in 1956. Its origin has much in common with that of the Manx National tartan in that the colours of the sett were symbolic of the 'district' which it was to represent. Following the success of the Nova Scotia tartan other provinces followed with designs of their own mainly based upon symbolism. New Brunswick (1959), Saskatchewan (1961), Manitoba (1962), Bruce County (1965) and British Columbia (1969) and Yukon (1984). Other tartans of the British Commonwealth are to be found in the Bahamas, Bermuda and Australia.

The subsequent growth of tartans in the United States was the consequence of the widespread role played by the Scottish organisations in the United States. One of the earliest is the American Bicentennial which was designed in conjunction with the Scottish Tartans Society in 1975. Its sett is intended to give the impression of the stars and stripes of the American national flag. It is now known as the 'American St Andrews'. The majority of the other USA tartans have also been designed either by, or in conjunction with the Scottish Tartans Society.

For example, in 1986 the Society created a tartan to commemorate the historical ties of the State of Georgia with Scotland. The design included components from the Royal Tartan and Government tartan in use at the time Georgia was founded in 1682.

In countries that do not have English or Gaelic as their mother tongue, a limited number of district tartans have been introduced. This book illustrates one from the Netherlands which was designed to commemorate the special association of the chiefs of the Clan Mackay with Holland.

The development of district tartans will undoubtedly continue wherever people wish to establish a means of common identity. It is the hope of the Scottish Tartans Society that new designs will be of a high quality. The Society's technical panel is always available to undertake original designs or to offer advice on those setts designed by others. It is in order to encourage high standards of design, and to maintain accurate historical records of the origin of a particular tartan, that the Council of the Scottish Tartans Society is willing to issue a 'Certificate of Accreditation' in respect of new tartans of quality (see p. 259).

# 'ROYAL' DISTRICT TARTANS

A few of the Scottish setts illustrated in subsequent pages have come to be known as the 'Royal' district tartans, particularly in the United States of America. This is because they were first known by the name of the royal dukedoms or earldoms to which they relate, for example, Fife and St Andrews respectively. Though some 'tartanologists', as students of tartan have been dubbed, would assert that such setts were personal to the holder of the title, there is a good case for regarding them as district tartans, whenever they are not already used as clan tartans.

Titles of nobility in many parts of the world are often associated with the territories which their bearers ruled over or owned, e.g. King of Serbia, Prince of Denmark, Count of Montecristo. In Scotland, titles have been directly associated with places from early times, particularly since the introduction of the feudal system by Anglo-Norman landowners. In the Gaelic tradition, a leader was known by his patronymic — *An Moireach Mor, Morair Ghallaobh, Mac Phadruig*. However, as the English language and the Anglo-Norman feudal system crept north, titles were conferred by the Crown to reflect territorial sovereignty. The Gaelic leaders above became known as 'Duke of Atholl (Murray), The Earl of Caithness (Sinclair), and Grant of Glenmoriston. Since chieftains and feudal leaders represented both the people and their place of residence, it was inevitable that clan and district tartans should complement each other.

The highest rank of peerage in the United Kingdom is that of duke. Except during the seventeenth and eighteenth centuries, new dukedoms have been bestowed almost exclusively on members of the royal family, or on those marrying into it. In the feudal period, the territory owned by a duke was considerable and in many cases remains so today. Ranking immediately below the title of duke is that of marquess followed by earl. The title of earl in Great Britain is equivalent to that of count in other parts of Europe. It originally related to the overlordship of the county or shire, hence the use of the title of countess by an earl's wife. In recent years, newly created earldoms have not implied actual lordship over the territories to which they

14

relate, and have been reserved for persons related to the monarch either by blood or marriage.

In Scotland, dukes, marquesses and earls have sometimes chosen to wear a tartan which represents their territorial title. For example, Augustus, Duke of Sussex (1773-1843), who was the son of George III, also bore the title of Earl of Inverness. In the latter role, he wore a red and blue tartan which he had specially woven. This is illustrated in James Logan's pioneer book on tartans, *The Scottish Gael*. This sett is now known as the Earl of Inverness tartan and is worn by some members of the royal family, the present earl being H.R.H. Prince Andrew. It is shared by the town and county of Inverness and is very popular. A similar regional representation has taken place with the tartan first designed for the Earl of St Andrews. This distinctive blue and white tartan reminiscent of the Scottish national flag, together with various items of clothing made from it, is sold in the shops of St Andrews as representative of the town. A number of other district tartans illustrated in this work are of 'royal' origin, woven first for a duke or earl bearing a title relating to the specific area. These include the Lennox, Lorne, Rothesay and Strathearn.

The adoption of a tartan bearing the territorial title of a distinguished 'royal' personage by people living within the district concerned may be perceived as an extension of the custom of followers wearing the tartan of their clan chief. This is a tradition which seems to have developed from the practice during the eighteenth century of certain chiefs and landowners supplying uniformly coloured tartan to the servitors on their estates, thus blurring the line between clan and district tartans. (See p. 8). Many such tartans were not, however, indigenous to the clan territory and were especially designed for a particular chief. Much the same is true of the 'royal' district tartans. Although they were originally created for individual members of the royal family, they are now identified also on sound historical grounds with the territories to which they relate. Conversely, their more general use may be regarded as a sign of respect towards the peer from which such tartans take their name. In *District Tartans* the 'royal' district tartans are so noted; their general simplicity, well-chosen patterns and colours, make them amongst the most beautiful of all tartans.

# AVAILABILITY OF DISTRICT TARTANS

Of the fifty-six Scottish district tartans illustrated in this book, approximately two-thirds are woven commercially and are available either from the weaving mills directly or through retail outlets around the world. Prospective purchasers should seek the tartan they wish from knowledgeable retailers who are willing to place an order for desired patterns. The Argyll may be purchased under the title Campbell of Cawdor, Buchan may be called Cumming, Hunting. Some mills currently weave limited stocks of lesser known district tartans like Arran or Strathspey while others may weave Gala Water and Nithsdale.

Some of the district tartans outwith Scotland can be obtained both from Scottish sources and in the areas with which they are associated. Scottish dealers routinely stock the Nova Scotia and other Commonwealth tartans. Cape Breton is seen in Scottish shops in the Maritimes while the Bermuda and Bahamas are popular in those holiday islands. The tartans of the Isle of Man are readily available on the island, as are those of Devon and Cornwall in their native counties. In every case, lengths of any tartan can be obtained through the Scottish Tartans Society.

District tartans not generally available can be obtained, on special order, through the Scottish Tartans Society at Pitlochry or the Scottish Tartan Museum at Comrie, Perthshire, Scotland. These will be more expensive than the more common tartans but given the uniqueness and durability make a good life-time investment. It is anticipated that the rising interest in district tartans will see more of them on the lists of tartan items readily available from retailers.

# THREAD COUNTS

Most tartans are of the reversing kind. The pattern begins at one 'pivot' and continues to a second 'pivot' after which it reverses with the colours in the same sequence and in the same proportions. The complete sett repeats itself both in warp and the weft, though it is important to remember that the 'pivot' at the end of the initial complete sett is also the beginning of the second and so on, that is the 'pivots' themselves do not duplicate at the beginning of the reverse. For example —

*Manx Dress*

| Half sett | **G** | B | Y | P | W | **G** | | | | | |
|---|---|---|---|---|---|---|---|---|---|---|---|
| | 8 | 34 | 4 | 16 | 56 | 8 | | | | | |
| Full sett | **G** | B | Y | P | W | **G** | W | P | Y | B | **G** |
| | 8 | 34 | 4 | 16 | 56 | 8 | 56 | 16 | 4 | 34 | 8 |

(The colours in bold type are the pivots)

In this book the thread counts shown in respect of each normal 'reversing' tartan are half setts from one pivot to the other.

The numbers given in a thread count are usually the number of threads in the sample from which they were taken. However, this does not mean that every time a tartan is woven the actual number of threads must be exactly as the thread count. It is the ratio of colours to one another which is important and providing this remains constant the number of threads in a tartan may be varied according to the type of cloth being woven.

A few tartans, however, are of a non-reversing type (asymmetric). These are tartans without the two pivots about which the pattern reverses. In such tartans at the end of the initial sequence of colours there is a second sequence, after which the first sequence is repeated in the same order, followed by the second sequence and so on without reversing. An example of such a tartan is the Ottawa (see p. 212).

Sometimes more than two sequences are used, although this has the effect of producing an exceedingly complicated and 'fuzzy' pattern. The thread counts of such tartans have to be given in full setts, numbered according to each section.

Another form of asymmetric tartan is when the warp and weft are different. This again is not usual, although such patterns were not unknown in early days since the hand weaver, having set up the warp, sometimes varied the number of threads in the weft, either deliberately or absent-mindedly. This produced material which, though constant in the warp, varied in the weft along its entire length.

The practice of verbally describing tartans by reference to colour blocks, e.g. the 'blue block' is a practice found probably more in Canada than in Scotland. The names refer to the predominant colours in each block and may be regarded as the background colour or 'field', upon which are those regarded as being crossed by lines or bands of different colours. If there are only two blocks, which alternate in the warp and weft the resultant tartan will be a normal reversing pattern providing each block has a central pivot on each side of which the colours appear in the same sequence and same proportions, each side being the mirror image of the other. If, however, the colours within each block do not have such a central pivot, the resulting tartan will be asymmetrical. This will also apply if there are more than two blocks.

In recent years there has been a tendency to refer to the normal reversing pattern as a true 'tartan' and the asymmetrical design as a 'plaid'.

# COLOUR ABBREVIATIONS

In recording a tartan sett, it is convenient to abbreviate the names of the colours rather than to spell them out in full. Two major systems are in use. One is that adopted by the Scottish Tartans Society for its master catalogue, Sindex, which forms part of the Register of All Publicly Known Tartans. The other is that used by the Lyon Court.

The Sindex abbreviations seek to use only one letter per colour, except in those cases in which there is more than one colour with the same initial letter. This method allows some discretion to the weaver in interpreting the choice of shades.

The Lyon Court system, concerned with the precision associated with the exact reproduction of a given pattern as part of heraldic grant-of-arms, uses longer abbreviations in an attempt to more closely define each colour shade.

In *District Tartans*, the Sindex system is used. Abbreviations and, in parenthesis, some of the logic used to determine each are listed below. For the basic colours there is one symbol for each. For tartan setts, where several shades of the same colour are used, prefixes are attached to show light, medium, or dark. In cases where an unusual shade or colour is recorded, the name is spelled in full.

| | | | |
|---|---|---|---|
| A | Azure | Mn | Maroon |
| B | Blue | N | Grey (Neutral) |
| C | Crimson or Rose | P | Purple |
| G | Green | R | Red |
| bK | Black | T | Brown (Tan) |
| Lv | Lavender | W | White |
| Ma | Magenta | Y | Yellow |

Prefixes:
L = Light    M = Medium    D = Dark
(Examples: LB for light blue, DR for dark red)

R = Royal as in RB (Royal Blue)
N = Navy as in NB (Navy Blue)
O = Olive as in OG (Olive Green)

In a few cases, where exact shades are important, prefixes can be used twice, as in LRB for Light Royal Blue.

It is recommended that the reader refer to this table when interpreting the thread/colour counts given in this book.

# The Scottish Tartans Society

SCOTTISH TARTANS SOCIETY

An Incorporation Noble in the Noblesse of Scotland Inaugurated on 13th May 1963 by Sir Thomas Innes of Learney, GCVO, Lord Lyon King of Arms 1945-1969.

BRING FORRIT THE TARTAN

## REGISTER OF ALL PUBLICLY KNOWN TARTANS

*Before Accreditation is granted the Register of All Publicly Known Tartans is searched to ensure that a tartan is original and unlikely to be confused with an existing tartan on the Register*

## CERTIFICATE OF ACCREDITATION

This is to certify that the

### East Kilbride Tartan

designed by Dr. Gordon Teall of Teallach

has been accredited by the

### Council of the Scottish Tartans Society

In witness whereof we the undersigned have affixed to this certificate no. 90008 our several signatures and the Common Seal of the Society

*Gordon Teall of Teallach*     Executive President

*Jimy Stewart*     Council Member

Dated this twentysixth     day of     June     1990

at the Scottish Tartans Society, Pitlochry, Perthshire, Scotland.

*Example of a Certificate of Accreditation issued by the Council of The Scottish Tartans Society (see p. 259).*

# SECTION II
# DISTRICT TARTANS
# OF SCOTLAND

## CONTENTS

| | | | |
|---|---|---|---|
| Aberdeen | 22 | Glen Tilt | 80 |
| Angus | 24 | Glen Trool | 82 |
| Applecross | 26 | Huntly | 84 |
| Argyll | 28 | Inverness | 86 |
| Arran | 30 | Largs | 88 |
| Atholl | 32 | Lennox | 90 |
| Ayrshire | 34 | Lochaber | 92 |
| Blairlogie | 36 | Loch Laggan | 94 |
| Buchan | 38 | Loch Rannoch | 96 |
| Caledonia | 40 | Lorne | 98 |
| Carrick | 42 | Mar | 100 |
| Crieff | 44 | Menteith | 102 |
| Culloden | 46 | Moffat | 104 |
| Cumbernauld | 48 | Mull | 106 |
| Deeside | 50 | Musselburgh | 108 |
| Dunbar | 52 | Nithsdale | 110 |
| Dunblane | 54 | Paisley | 112 |
| Dundee | 56 | Perthshire | 114 |
| East Kilbride | 58 | Rothesay | 116 |
| Edinburgh | 60 | Roxburgh | 118 |
| Eglinton | 62 | St Andrews | 120 |
| Ettrick | 64 | Stirling and | |
| Fife | 66 | Bannockburn | 122 |
| Fort William | 68 | Strathclyde | 124 |
| Gala Water | 70 | Strathearn | 126 |
| Galloway | 72 | Strathspey | 128 |
| Glasgow | 74 | Sutherland | 130 |
| Glen Lyon | 76 | Tweedside | 132 |
| Glen Orchy | 78 | | |

# ABERDEEN

*Gaelic Name*

## Obair Dheathain

*Designers* Wilsons of Bannockburn

*Date* pre 1794

Aberdeen, the city at the mouth (aber) of the River Dee, is famous for its cathedral and university, the 'Granite City' is the commercial and intellectual centre of the rich farmlands of the east coast. Aberdeen is Britain's third largest fishing port and is today the major terminus of the North Sea oil industry.

The Aberdeen district tartan has a very complex pattern having 446 'threads' in the half sett. A full repeat in modern weave would span approximately twenty-two inches which is more than the width of the apron of a modern kilt (feileadh-beag). It seems likely, therefore, that when the pattern was originally woven, it was intended for use as a plaid or blanket sett, probably for shawls, but possibly for the great kilt (feileadh-mor).

An order, dated 20 June 1794 addressed to the renowned weavers William Wilson and Sons of Bannockburn, from Scott and Anderson, is probably the earliest written reference to this tartan. It was mentioned again in the Wilsons records in 1795 and subsequently appeared in their manuscript list of 1800 and their 1819 Key Pattern Book.

There is evidence to suggest that Wilsons themselves believed that the sett was introduced and named by them during the period 1746-1782 when tartan was proscribed by law. The Aberdeen tartan is certainly one of Scotland's oldest district tartans.

| W | G | bK | W | P | A | W | A | P | W | P | R | C | W | C | R |
|---|---|---|---|---|---|---|---|---|---|---|---|---|---|---|---|
| 4 | 8 | 32 | 4 | 12 | 8 | 4 | 8 | 12 | 4 | 6 | 16 | 6 | 4 | 6 | 16 |
| P | W | bK | G | bK | W | P | R | C | W | C | R | P | W | A | W |
| 6 | 4 | 24 | 8 | 24 | 4 | 6 | 16 | 6 | 4 | 6 | 16 | 6 | 4 | 20 | 2 |
| R | C | W | C | R | W | C | bK | W | R | C | **W** | | | | |
| 12 | 6 | 2 | 6 | 12 | 2 | 8 | 32 | 4 | 46 | 6 | 4 | | | | |

# ANGUS

*Gaelic Name*

**Aonghas**

*Designer* Unknown

*Date* 1906 (or earlier)

The fertile Braes of Angus drain into the River Isla along Strathmore, the 'Great Valley' that skirts the southeast edge of the Central Highlands. A former county (previously called Forfarshire), Angus has since 1975 been a District in Tayside Region. The Earldom of Angus, one of the most ancient in Scotland, is now vested in the Dukedom of Hamilton. The name 'Gilchrist' has stayed in Angus as one of the names of Clan Ogilvie, whose Chief, the Earl of Airlie, represents a family granted lands in Angus about 1172. The Scottish nobles met in April 1320, in Angus at Arbroath, to declare that, '. . . for so long as a hundred remain alive we are minded never a whit to bow beneath the yoke of English dominion.'

Angus tartan first appeared in Messrs W. & A. K. Johnston's *The Tartans of the Clans and Septs of Scotland*, published in two volumes in 1906. Its origin is unknown and it is not clear whether or not it was originally intended as a family or district tartan. In consequence, it has been used as both. In the context of this book it is now firmly established as a tartan for all those people having a connection with Angus.

| bK | R | bK | B | R | B | R | B | R |
|----|---|----|---|---|---|---|---|---|
| 6 | 2 | 64 | 56 | 2 | 4 | 2 | 4 | 6 |

# APPLECROSS

*Gaelic Name*

## A'Chomraich

*Designer* Unknown

*Date* 1947 (or earlier)

This sparsely settled peninsula is still one of the remoter regions of the Highlands. Facing Skye across the Inner Sound from Wester Ross, Applecross is still Gaelic speaking and even today is accessible only by secondary roads. Its beauty and solitude appeals to many visitors. Applecross is an anglicised form of an old Pictish name, but the district is traditionally known in Gaelic as *A'Chomraich*, 'the sanctuary'.

This sett is to be found in Messrs W. Anderson's collection in 1947. It is very similar to that of the red 'Lord of the Isle and Sleat' as recorded by Johnson. It has apparently been named after the district in which it was found. Although Applecross is traditionally in MacKenzie country, that family has never been associated with this tartan and there is little doubt that the tartan is MacDonald in origin. There were MacDonald lands just south of Applecross on Loch Carron and on Skye.

| **G** | R | G | **R** |
|---|---|---|---|
| 72 | 8 | 28 | 72 |

# ARGYLL

*Gaelic Name*

## Earraghaidheal

*Designer* Unknown
(included in records of Wilsons of Bannockburn)

*Date* 1819 (probably earlier)

Argyll the 'high land of the Gael', is the part of Scotland that points like the fingers of a hand south across the sea to Ireland. Only twelve miles separate the Mull of Kintyre and the coast of Ulster. Around the fifth century, the Gaels moved east to Carrick and Galloway and north to Argyll where they founded the Kingdom of Dalriada. Expanding north and east through Argyll, the Scots assimilated the earlier Picts and brought their language and culture to all of the north of Scotland. Argyll is a land of green peninsulas, high mountains, fertile valleys and majestic lochs. Argyll is often identified with the Campbells, whose chief is the Duke of Argyll.

The first record of the Argyll district tartan is in the 1819 Key Pattern Book of Wilsons of Bannockburn when it is referred to as 'No. 230 or Argyll'. Amongst this firm's accounts for 1798 there is an 'Argyll tartan' mentioned and, though one cannot be certain, this may well have been the same sett. W. & S. Smith were the first to illustrate this tartan in their 1850 publication in which it is called 'Cawdor Campbell'. They give the Earl of Cawdor as their source and it is reasonable to conclude that the sett was accepted as 'Campbell of Cawdor' by that date. The pattern was worn by the 91st Argyllshire Highlanders as 'Campbell' between 1865-81. As a consequence it became identified with the County of Argyll, from the inhabitants of which the regiment was raised. In W. & A. K. Johnston's *The Tartans of the Clans and Septs of Scotland* in the text to 'Dunblane', the Campbell of Cawdor tartan is called 'Argyll District tartan'. This sett has a feeling of being a truly old one, since it is similar to several patterns from other parts of the west coast and islands.

| A | bK | G | bK | B | bK | R |
|---|----|----|----|----|----|----|
| 4 | 2 | 16 | 16 | 16 | 2 | 4 |

# ARRAN

*Gaelic Name*

**Arainn**

*Designer* MacNaughtons of Pitlochry

*Date* 1982

Arran, the large mountainous island in the Firth of Clyde, rises steeply from the sea. Easily visible from many places on the Scottish mainland and from Ireland, Arran is a conspicuous landmark which has long since captured the hearts of visitors. Early settlers included Christian ascetics and some of its place-names reflect the Viking era. The history of Arran is essentially one of tenant farmers, generations following generation, to modern times. Gaelic was spoken on the island until well into this century. It has long been a popular tourist resort and at one time many businessmen used to commute from Arran to offices in Glasgow by ferry and rail. Visitors to the island still arrive by ferry to challenge the steep hills, while the gardens of Brodick Castle, now in care of the National Trust for Scotland, attract the more leisurely visitor.

The Arran district tartan is a modern sett introduced by MacNaughtons of Pitlochry in 1982. It has recently been produced with a colour modification by Lochcarron Mills at Galashiels.

| **P** | N | P | N | P | bK | R | bK | R | bK | R | bK | R | W |
|-----|---|---|---|---|----|---|----|---|----|---|----|----|---|
| 178 | 8 | 8 | 8 | 8 | 32 | 4 | 8  | 6 | 6  | 8 | 4  | 10 | 6 |

| R | bK | R | bK | R | bK | R | bK | N | bK | **N** |
|----|----|---|----|---|----|---|----|---|----|-----|
| 10 | 4  | 8 | 6  | 6 | 8  | 4 | 32 | 42 | 8 | 20 |

# ATHOLL

*Gaelic Name*

**Athall**

*Designer* Wilsons of Bannockburn

*Date* 1812

Atholl, a large basin on the south slope of the Grampian Mountains drains into the River Garry and Glen Garry. The historic route from Perthshire to Inverness enters Atholl through the gorge of Killiecrankie, the site of the defeat in 1689 of the government forces under General Mackay by John Graham of Claverhouse, Viscount Dundee, with his Highlanders. Home of the Stewarts, Robertsons and Murrays, Atholl is today seeing a resurgence of interest in its history. Blair Castle, home of the Duke of Atholl, houses one of the most complete collection of Highland weapons and armour to be found anywhere. Further north, Clan Robertson has opened a Clan Museum.

The Atholl district tartan is one of the oldest. There may be a reference to it as early as 1619. When the Black Watch was formed the men apparently wore two tartans — the Government or Black Watch tartan for the long breacan-feile and the Atholl tartan for the little kilt, the feileadh-beag. In the early 1800s the sett was worn as a district tartan by the Chief of the Robertsons. More recently, the early tartan, with its distinctive red stripe has been identified with the northern Murrays and is today sold as Murray of Atholl.

It was recorded in 1812 (W.P.B. Appendix 1802).

The present Duke of Atholl, Ian Murray, President of the Scottish Tartans Society, has stated that he is very happy for the Murray of Atholl tartan to be regarded as the Atholl district tartan.

| **B** | bK | B | bK | B | bK | G | R | G | bK | B | bK | **R** |
|----|----|----|----|----|----|----|----|----|----|----|----|----|
| 24 | 4 | 4 | 4 | 4 | 24 | 24 | 6 | 24 | 24 | 24 | 2 | 6 |

# AYRSHIRE

*Gaelic Name*

## Siorrachd Air

*Designer* Dr Philip D. Smith F.S.T.S.

*Date* 1988

Ayrshire looks across the Firth of Clyde to the Island of Arran and the Mull of Kintyre. Ayrshire has often been the first part of Scotland seen by the international traveller, sailing up the Clyde by ship in times past or later on arrival at the International Airport at Prestwick. Few visitors tarry, much to their own loss, to see more of Ayrshire in detail. A long-established agricultural area of smaller towns, Ayshire has given its name to a noted strain of dairy cattle. Robert Burns, the most famous of Scotland's sons, was born and lived most of his life here. Burns was proud of his Ayrshire background and wrote of himself as 'Robin ... born in Kyle' (a district in the area). Although he died in Dumfries, Burns is buried in Alloway.

Part of the early British-speaking Kingdom of Strathclyde, Ayrshire was later partially Gaelic-speaking until the mid-eighteenth century. The shire's rich history is linked to the fortunes of the Stewarts, Cunninghams, Hamiltons and Boyds. Today castles and ruins abound while the rugged coast and offshore islands are favourites of photographers. Seaside village resorts attract knowledgeable visitors and Kilmarnock and Irvine are its busy modern urban centres.

The Ayrshire tartan as designed by Dr Philip Smith at the suggestion of the Clan Boyd and Clan Cunningham Societies as an alternative tartan for Ayrshire families and friends. It reflects the gold of the rising sun, the green of the land and brown of the coast, the blue of the sea and the red of the setting sun. The Ayrshire tartan is intended for those with connections in the districts of Kyle, Cunninghame, and Inverclyde.

| B | R | B | W | T | G | Y | G |
|---|---|---|---|---|---|---|---|
| 4 | 2 | 20 | 2 | 8 | 16 | 2 | 4 |

# BLAIRLOGIE

*Gaelic Name*

**Blar Lagaidh**

*Designer* Unknown

*Date* c.1882

Blairlogie is a small village within sight of the Wallace Monument. The main street is a turning off the road from Alva to Stirling. It winds, in part, along the side of a small burn, until it reaches the Square, around which stand flower-decked houses. Beyond the square, a private road leads to the Castle, which nestles beneath the broom-covered crags of Dumyat and overlooks the plain of the River Forth. The Castle was built in 1543 as a single tower by Alexander Spittle, whose grandson, Adam, added a wing in 1582. To this day, the Castle bears the initials of the builder and his wife Elizabeth Hay.

The Blairlogie tartan is of complex design and three thread counts are recorded in the Register of All Publicly Known Tartans, all of which have the same sequence of colours, but in varying proportions. Two of the counts are identical apart from the pivots. One of these is given below and in the other, known as the original, the blue pivot contains only 4 threads and the black 40. The third sett differs significantly with regard to the widths of the seventeen colour bands (*B*8 R2 B20 G6 B10 G50 bK2 G2 W6 bK2 G50 B10 G6 B20 R6 *bK* 80). In this case, the extra large number of threads in each pivot probably came about by a weaver mistakenly following the former, now discarded, practice of doubling the pivot figures given in a thread count when setting up his loom. The Blairlogie tartan was rediscovered amongst the records of D.C. Dalgleish (Weavers) of Selkirk in March 1967, by a member of the Scottish Tartans Society. It is thought to date from c.1882.

| **B** | R | B | G | B | G | bK | G | W | G | bK | G | B | G |
|---|---|---|---|---|---|---|---|---|---|---|---|---|---|
| 6 | 2 | 16 | 4 | 8 | 38 | 2 | 2 | 4 | 2 | 2 | 38 | 8 | 4 |

| B | R | **bK** |
|---|---|---|
| 16 | 4 | 56 |

# BUCHAN

*Gaelic Name*

**Buchan**

*Designer* Unknown

*Date* c.1790 (or earlier)

Buchan is the northeast tip of central Scotland. It has generally been free from foreign incursions and alarms but has a long history of local feuds and forays. It is a land devoted to fishing and farming.

The Buchan district tartan is one of the oldest named setts. It is asymetric and rather complex. Originally, it appears to have been a district tartan for the Glenorchy area in the West. The earliest sample, on loan to the Scottish Tartans Society, is a nineteenth-century cushion cover made of vegetable-dyed material woven by hand in about 1790. The same pattern is to be found in the Collection of the Highland Society of London, now in the care of the National Museum of Scotland. Dating from about 1816, the sample is labelled 'MacIntyre and Glenorchy', the MacIntyres being a prominent family in the Glenorchy area. In *The Clans of the Highlands of Scotland* (1850) Thomas Smibert depicts a slightly different and extended sett, which is named 'Cumming and Glenorchy', also taken from the Highland Society Collection.

In about 1965, the Buchan family adopted the sett on account of their long association with the Cummings which began with the second marriage, c.1210, of Margaret, the daughter of King Edgar, to William Coymen, sheriff of Forfar. By her first marriage she was the Countess of Buchan. The present chief of the Buchans is Captain David Buchan of Auchmacoy, the earldom having now passed to the Erskines. The name Buchan, though a family name, is territorial in origin, probably deriving from Gaelic *bo-chain* ('cow tribute'). It is, therefore, an interesting tribute to the family of Buchan that the former Glenorchy district tartan is now accepted as the Buchan district tartan.

| B | bK | R | G | R | bK | R | G | R | bK | B | R | bK | R |
|---|----|---|---|---|----|---|---|---|----|---|---|----|---|
| 4 | 12 | 4 | 54 | 4 | 4 | 4 | 54 | 4 | 12 | 12 | 4 | 48 | 4 |

| B | bK | R | bK | R | G | R ... |
|---|----|---|----|---|---|-------|
| 4 | 4 | 4 | 48 | 4 | 12 | 12 |

# CALEDONIA

*Designer* Unknown

*Date* Probably eighteenth century, or earlier

No book on district tartans would be complete without the colourful Caledonia tartan. The very name Caledonia conjures up pictures of Roman soldiers striding northwards towards the land of mountains, lochs, forest and glens they failed to subdue. To sailors, the Caledonian Canal, cutting through the Great Glen from Loch Linnhe to the Moray Firth, encapsulates so much of what is typical of Highland Scotland.

The 'Caledonia' tartan was popular in the eighteenth century and appears in a number of guises. Romantic stories are told of its origin but in reality little is definitely known. It is a suitable tartan for anyone who wishes to be associated with Scotland and is the choice of a number of pipe bands.

The sett given below is an early one and is taken from the Wilsons of Bannockburn Pattern Book of 1819 (No. 155).

| **R** | A | bK | A | bK | A | bK | Y | G | R | bK | R | W | **R** |
|----|----|----|----|----|----|----|----|----|----|----|----|----|----|
| 42 | 18 | 4 | 4 | 4 | 18 | 36 | 6 | 42 | 26 | 6 | 26 | 4 | 26 |

# CARRICK

*Gaelic Name*

## Carraig

*Designer* Arthur Galt

*Date* c.1930

Carrick, the ancient Earldom on the west coast of southern Scotland, is a land of rolling hills and rich farms. It formed part of Ayrshire which is now incorporated in Strathclyde Region, and it gives its name to the District of Kyle and Carrick. Somewhat higher than its neighbouring districts, Carrick looks directly across to Ireland. Carrick has not yet lost the character that it maintained throughout the thousand years it was a major sub-division of Scotland. Robert the Bruce began his rise to the throne as Earl of Carrick. Two major families are identified with Carrick: Ferguson and Kennedy. The Kennedys' first stronghold was their castle at Dunure and their subsequent seat, Culzean Castle, is now one of the most famous of the National Trust for Scotland properties. 'Carrick' is a territorial name derived from the Gaelic word for 'rock', 'carraig', and may refer to the offshore island of Ailsa Craig. The Carrick 'Red' district tartan was designed in about 1930 for Councillor John Hannay by Arthur Galt of Messrs. Hugh Galt & Sons Ltd., of Barrhill, Girvan.

There is an alternative sett, which was produced at the same time, known as 'Carrick Green' (G26 P2 G2 P2 G6 B10 bK8 Y4).

| **R** | B | R | G | P | G | P | G | **R** |
|-------|-----|-----|-----|-----|-----|-----|-----|-------|
| 56 | 24 | 6 | 40 | 2 | 4 | 2 | 4 | 14 |

# CRIEFF

*Gaelic Name*

## Craoibh

*Designer* Unknown (included in Wilsons Records)

*Date* c.1793

The medieval town cross still stands in the centre of this ancient trading town of Strathearn. Built on the hillside overlooking the rich lands of the Drummond estates, Crieff apparently began as a place where Highlander and Lowlander could meet and trade. The town takes its name from the Gaelic *craobh*, 'tree'. Legends vary — this may be a reference to a 'hanging tree' or simply recognition of the richness of the woodland in the area. Crieff was the most famous of the annual cattle drovers' and buyers' 'trysts' until these moved south to Falkirk in the 1700s. Highlanders Loan ('Lane') just east of the town commemorates the drovers' route south from Breadalbane down Glen Almond to the open country of the Earn. The modern town is noted for its beautiful setting overlooking Strathearn and for its fine hotels, a popular place for holidays.

There is a mention, with no details of the Crieff district tartan in the accounts of Wilsons of Bannockburn dated 1793. In a manuscript of the same firm dated 1800, it is quoted in quantities of colour but no actual scale is given. The count below is taken from Wilsons Key Pattern Book of 1819.

| C | R | G | R | G | R | P | R | G | R | G | R | C |
|---|---|---|---|---|---|---|---|---|---|---|---|---|
| 4 | 12 | 8 | 140 | 8 | 4 | 42 | 4 | 170 | 4 | 8 | 12 | 4 |

# CULLODEN

*Gaelic Name*
## Cuil-lodair
*Designer* Unknown
*Date* 1746 (or earlier)

Culloden, the last land battle on British soil, was fought near a farm on Drummossie Muir outside Inverness on 16 April 1746. It signalled the end of both the Jacobite cause and the Highland clan system. Here the small Jacobite army under Prince Charles Edward (Highlanders, Irish and Lowland Jacobites) were defeated by a larger, better equipped, and better led force of regulars and Scottish militia under the Duke of Cumberland. The end of the 'Forty-Five' rising brought proscription of the tartan and, even more long-lasting, laws which restricted the power of the clan chiefs and ended an entire way of life. The 'Culloden' tartan was worn by a member of Prince Charles's staff during the battle but it is not known with which family or district it was first connected. It was first illustrated in *Old and Rare Scottish Tartans*, 1893 by D. W. Stewart who commented that —

> 'Despite an uncommon and daring colour scheme, the general result is pleasing and effective.'

His son, D. C. Stewart, one of the founder members of the Scottish Tartan Society, in his book *Setts of the Scottish Tartans* wrote —

> 'We have seen that highly complex tartans were in vogue at the time of the final crash of Jacobite hopes, and here we have one which shows that the Highland love of exuberant colour could express itself with admirable taste.'

Although the Culloden tartan has no direct link with the local population, it has now become firmly established as the district tartan for the area.

A number of modern 'dress' Culloden tartans have been designed recently which many women find attractive for evening wear.

| R | A | P | W | bK | DY | B | Y |
|---|---|----|---|----|----|---|---|
| 10 | 4 | 28 | 4 | 26 | 26 | 4 | 6 |

# CUMBERNAULD

*Designer* Frank Gordon

*Date* 1987

Cumbernauld is one of Scotland's most successful new towns. It is a centre for new industries and has a special place in the developing technologies of modern Scotland. The Cumbernauld area was selected and designated a new town centre in 1956. At that time, it consisted of the three small villages of Cumbernauld, Castlecary and Condorrat, together with their surrounding hills and countryside. The villages stood midway on the narrow waist between the Forth and the Clyde, and thus midway between Edinburgh and Glasgow, Scotland's two great commercial and industrial cities. All three villages remain in the green, open new town of today and their features add to the character of a unique environment. The new town centre is situated on a hilltop encircled by self-contained neighbourhoods and nearby lies the Palacerigg Country Park.

Sponsored by Cumbernauld Development Corporation for the purpose of promoting the town and for the use of its citizens, the 'Cumbernauld' tartan was designed by a local man, Frank Gordon, a well-known kiltmaker from Condorrat, Cumbernauld. Mr Gordon based the tartan on the Government tartan, incorporating ancient and modern colours to depict the emergence of a new thriving community, proud of its heritage. The tartan has been accredited by the Scottish Tartans Society and is entered in the register of All Publicly Known Tartans.

| R | bK | DB | bK | G | bK | W | bK | G | bK | DB | bK | DB | bK | DB |
|---|----|----|----|----|----|----|----|----|----|----|----|----|----|----|
| 6 | 6 | 34 | 34 | 34 | 4 | 6 | 4 | 34 | 34 | 6 | 6 | 6 | 6 | 34 |

# DEESIDE

*Gaelic Name*
**Strath Dhe**

*Designer* Fenton Wynes
*Date* 1963

There are two rivers with the name Dee in Scotland; One in the Grampian Region in the northeast, the other in Dumfries and Galloway in the southwest. It is to the former that the Deeside district tartan relates. The northern Deeside is an extensive area since the river Dee drains some 765 square miles of countryside, mainly in the former county of Aberdeenshire. The river rises in a spring on Braeriach, one of the peaks in the Cairngorms, 4061 feet in height, with a secondary source, the Pools of Dee in the Lairig Ghru. Its initial course flows southwards through the wild, steep-sided Glen Dee, until it joins the Geldie Burn at White Bridge. Thence it turns eastwards through Aberdeen. Wooded slopes flank the river in many places. It is not surprising that Queen Victoria chose it as the site for her Scottish home, Balmoral. The names of many of its towns and villages are known throughout the Highland world because of their Highland Games. Braemar, always attended by the Royal Family, Ballater, Aboyne, Banchory and Aberdeen, among them. Deeside, too is renowned for its fine salmon fishing.

The Deeside district tartan was designed in 1963 by a well-known local historian and architect from Aberdeen, Fenton Wynes, on behalf of the Dee Valley Textiles Ltd. The tartan is symbolic, which is unusual for Scottish district tartans. The colours represent —

| | |
|---|---|
| Grey | the granite rocks and pinnacles and enshrouding mists |
| Blue | the River Dee and the two great mountain ranges, the Grampians and Cairngorms |
| Green | the pine forests, the Scots firs and larches |
| White | the slender birch trunks and the snow in remote corries |
| Yellow | the broom, gorse and the bracken |
| Purple | the heather, bell and ling and the Royal Purple for the Celtic dynasties and their present-day successors, the House of Windsor |

| **W** | N | P | N | G | B | **Y** |
|---|---|---|---|---|---|---|
| 4 | 4 | 10 | 30 | 4 | 20 | 4 |

# DUNBAR

*Designer* Wilsons of Bannockburn

*Date* c.1860

Dunbar is one of the few ports on Scotland's southeast coast. Though small, it has been of great strategic value from earliest times since invading armies, which travelled up the coastal roads, were supplied by sea. Twice Dunbar saw the defeat of defending Scottish armies; by the English in 1296 and also in 1650 when Cromwell defeated troops loyal to Charles II under General Leslie. Today Dunbar is a modern fishing and industrial town as well as a seasonal resort twenty-seven miles east of Edinburgh. Its church of red sandstone is a familiar landmark to those travelling by rail on the east-coast main line from London to Edinburgh.

The very simple Dunbar district tartan is quite distinct from the red and green sett of the Dunbar family, who owned lands to the west. It was first reported by MacGregor Hastie in 1934, who noted a specimen on loan to Kinloch Anderson Ltd. in Edinburgh. It was regarded there as being one of the setts produced by Wilsons of Bannockburn. In a report addressed to the Scottish Tartans Society in 1970, D. C. Stewart challenged the association of this sett both with the name Dunbar and with that of Wilsons. Research conducted by 1982 by Gerry Newnham, a member of the Council of the Scottish Tartans Society, however, indicated that the tartan had its origin in the nineteenth-century Wilsons Pattern Book (Ref. B59 62/J). He noted in the archives of the Smiths Institute at Stirling a non-reversing Dunbar tartan. The similarity between the two can be seen when a half sett of this non-reversing tartan is compared with a full sett of the present Dunbar district tartan.

| *Non-reversing Dunbar tartan* | | | | | |
|---|---|---|---|---|---|
| bK | W | bK | Y | bK | R |
| 16 | 6 | 40 | 6 | 16 | 98..... |

| *Dunbar district* | | | | | | |
|---|---|---|---|---|---|---|
| **R** | bK | W | **bK** | W | bK | **R** |
| 56 | 8 | 4 | 26 | 4 | 8 | 56 |

# DUNBLANE

*Gaelic Name*
**Dun Blathain**
*Designer* Unknown
*Date* Pre 1729

Dunblane is a small town on the Allan Water just five miles north of Stirling. Nearby are the remains of the Roman Camp at Ardoch. This still unexcavated site was the largest Roman camp in Britain, covering many acres. From this base small Roman garrisons and signal stations skirted the Highland Line from Comrie at the narrows of Strathearn north to Taymouth. Dunblane Cathedral dates from the thirteenth century and was restored from a ruined state in the late nineteenth. The town today is both a tourist centre and home to commuters from Edinburgh and Glasgow, each an hour away by car or rail.

The Dunblane tartan is said to be taken from a portrait at Hornby Castle, Yorkshire, of Peregrine, 2nd Viscount Dunblane, who died in 1729, thus making it one of the earliest known setts. It was revived in 1822 on the occasion of the visit of George IV to Scotland.

It is recorded in the work of W. & A. Smith, 1850.

| **G** | Y | W | G | W | G | W | G | W | R | B | **W** |
|----|----|----|----|----|----|----|----|----|----|----|----|
| 12 | 10 | 2 | 4 | 2 | 10 | 2 | 4 | 2 | 30 | 4 | 2 |

# DUNDEE

*Gaelic Name*

**Dun Deagh**

*Designer* Wilsons of Bannockburn

*Date* Pre 1819

Dundee, a port city on the Firth of Tay, is one of Scotland's major industrial centres. Built on the slope of Dundee Law, the city has always been the focus of trade for a large area. For a time it was the leading centre for the manufacture of jute. This trade has been replaced by a diversity of industries and Dundee is currently Scotland's leader in electronic and laser technology. It is also a university city. The stirring march, 'Bonnie Dundee' commemorates not the city but John Graham of Claverhouse, Viscount Dundee.

The late John Cargill of Dundee, one of the early members of the Scottish Tartans Society, considered that the Dundee tartan was first woven at the end of the eighteenth century, or early in the nineteenth by Wilsons of Bannockburn. The weaving scale is preserved in the Key Pattern Book of that firm dated 1819. The actual design of the tartan is very similar to that of a tartan jacket said to have been worn by Prince Charles Edward Stuart at the Battle of Culloden in 1746. This jacket is now preserved in the Scottish United Services Museum in Edinburgh Castle.

| **W** | P | W | A | Y | W | P | W | Y | G | C | bK | C | **R** |
|----|----|----|----|----|----|----|----|----|----|----|----|----|----|
| 12 | 12 | 4 | 14 | 8 | 4 | 4 | 4 | 8 | 44 | 4 | 30 | 4 | 84 |

# EAST KILBRIDE

*Gaelic Name*

## Cille Bhrighde an Ear

*Designer* Dr D.G. Teall of Teallach F.S.T.S. for the Scottish
Tartans Society

*Date* 1990

East Kilbride is situated some twelve miles south of Glasgow.
Formerly, a large village, it was designated as the first of
Scotland's new towns and is now a thriving industrial community, with new factories and businesses. Many of the present
inhabitants have moved to the town from Glasgow.

In 1990, the East Kilbride Development Corporation decided to
encapsulate the community spirit of the new town in an
especially commissioned tartan. This was designed by Dr
Gordon Teall of Teallach on behalf of the Scottish Tartans
Society. The tartan has red as its predominant colour and the
secondary colours have been chosen to echo the symbolism of
the ensigns armorial granted by the Lord Lyon King of Arms as
follows —

| | |
|---|---|
| White/Silver and Blue | Stewarts of Torrance |
| White/Silver and Black | Maxwells of Calderwood |
| Red and White | Lindsays |
| White/Silver and Black | Industry |
| Green and Gold | Agriculture |

The colours and various features of the proposed East Kilbride
District tartan are to be found also in the tartans indirectly
associated with East Kilbride — Gordon, Maxwell, Stewart
and Lindsay. In particular, the yellow stripe of the Gordon sett
appears in the East Kilbride tartan to commemorate the first
provost, John Gordon. A rug made from the East Kilbride
tartan was presented to H.M. The Queen on her official visit to
East Kilbride in 1990.

| **W** | bK | R | B | G | R | **Y** |
|---|---|---|---|---|---|---|
| 4 | 2 | 30 | 20 | 14 | 20 | 6 |

# EDINBURGH

*Gaelic Name*
## Dun Eideann

*Designer* Councillor Hugh Macpherson

*Date* 1970

Edinburgh, the historic capital of Scotland, has been called the 'Athens of the North' because it too has a series of hills and a long dedication to learning and the arts. In earliest times, men built a defensive position on the high steep rock that dominates the skyline. With the southern expansion of the Kingdom of the Scots Edinburgh became the principal residence of the monarch and, eventually, the capital city. It was extended in the late 1700s with the addition of the Georgian 'New Town', now the central area of Edinburgh.

The Castle looms above a modern city remarkable for its richness of history and culture. Visitors can see St Margaret's Chapel, the oldest building there and still hear the cannon signal the hour at 1 pm. Recent excavations nearby have shown evidence that the Romans once occupied the castle site. The Edinburgh Festival and the Tattoo are favourites of visitors from all over the world. There are numerous museums in the city and it is the home of one of the world's great universities.

Several attempts have been made to develop a special tartan for residents or visitors. None had success until the design of the Edinburgh tartan by Councillor Hugh Macpherson on behalf of Hugh Macpherson Ltd. in 1970 on the occasion of the Commonwealth Games. It is symbolic and represents the colours of Edinburgh as follows —

| | |
|---|---|
| Black | The city's colours and the school colours of the Royal High |
| White | ditto |
| Maroon | George Watsons and Hearts F.C. |
| Green | Hibs. F.C., Holy Cross Academy and by adding black, Boroughmuir |
| Blue | Edinburgh Academy, Heriots, Portobello Secondary and Edinburgh Curling Club |
| Scarlet | Complementary to some of the above colours |

| W | B | Mn | C | Mn | C | G | Mn | bK |
|---|---|----|---|----|---|---|----|----|
| 6 | 50 | 6 | 6 | 6 | 10 | 20 | 6 | 4 |

# EGLINTON

*Designer* Unknown

*Date* Pre 1847

Eglinton Castle and village stand on Lugton Water between Irvine and Kilwinning on the coast of Ayrshire. The imposing structure is a typical Scottish stronghold. The port of Ardrossan, some six miles to the west, owed its origin to the endeavours of an Earl of Eglinton who constructed extensive harbour works in 1806 in connection with a proposed canal to Glasgow. This scheme did not materialise, but a railway, built to the Kilwinning coalmines in 1827, brought prosperity.

Eglinton is the seat of the Montgomeries, earls of Eglinton, who were for centuries the dominant family of western Ayrshire. D. W. Stewart was of the opinion that the Montgomerie tartan was adopted by the Montgomeries of Ayrshire in 1707, about the time of the Act of Union between England and Scotland. He stated that in 1893 there were historic relics at Eglinton Castle which furnished evidence of the early use of this tartan. The Eglinton tartan is the Montgomerie tartan with a narrower ground and was first recorded in Wilsons of Bannockburn book No. 4, c1847, with the alternative description of No. 7.

| **bK** | G | bK | A | bK | R | **bK** |
|--------|---|----|----|----|----|--------|
| 6 | 6 | 6 | 32 | 6 | 6 | 6 |

# ETTRICK

*Designer* Unknown

*Date* c.1900

The Ettrick valley, formerly in the county of Selkirk, now forms part of the Ettrick and Lauderdale District Council in the Borders Region, established in 1975 under a local government act. Ettrick Forest covers a large area and was a favourite hunting ground for the Royal House of Stewart. Sheep-raising, encouraged particularly by James V, led to virtually the complete destruction of the old forest of birch and oak, and the area today is mainly pastoral although in recent years many young plantations have been established. It is a sparsely populated area of uplands with 'laws', 'rigs' and 'knowes' rising to 2000 feet and above. One of the highest hills is Ettrick Pen, 2270 feet, the western slopes of which drain into the Ettrick Water, which eventually flows into the River Tweed near Selkirk. In Ettrick churchyard are buried Thomas Boston, exponent of Calvinism theology; James Hogg, the 'Ettrick Shepherd', poet and novelist; and Tibbie Shiel, who kept the famous inn at St Mary's Loch.

The precise circumstances relating to the design of the Ettrick tartan are not known, but it was included in Book 4 of Wilsons of Bannockburn, Pattern Collections, dated c.1900. It is a very simple design in black and red.

**bK**  R  bK  **R**
20  104  104  20

# FIFE

*Gaelic Name*

**Fiobha**

*Designer* Unknown

*Date* 1889

Fife, the low-lying rich farmland of the wide peninsula between the Firths of Forth and Tay, has been a major source of Scotland's agricultural wealth since prehistoric times. Separated from the rest of the mainland by the Ochil Hills and Lomond Hills, the Kingdom of Fife is one of Scotland's early political divisions. Traces of Bronze Age settlements stand beside Roman ruins, medieval churches and modern towns. Fife is noted for its distinctive coastline and many picturesque small towns and fishing ports.

The tartan illustrated is known as the 'Duke of Fife' and was designed for the celebration of the wedding in 1889 of Louise, the Princess Royal, daughter of Edward VII, granddaughter of Queen Victoria, to Alexander Duff, the first Duke of Fife. One of the earliest samples of the fabric is to be found in the late nineteenth-century pattern book of Fraser, Ross & Co., of Glasgow, though the thread count (*G64* bK12 G8 bK16 R2 *bK4*), differs somewhat from that used today.

In recent years, this commemorative tartan has come to be regarded as a district tartan for Fife. Such a transposition of purpose, however, is not necessarily unacceptable providing the historical background is understood and it is not suggested that originally it was an old district sett of the Kingdom of Fife.

| G | bK | G | bK | R | bK |
|---|---|---|---|---|---|
| 24 | 12 | 4 | 8 | 4 | 6 |

# FORT WILLIAM

*Gaelic Name*

## An Gearsadan

*Designer* Wilsons of Bannockburn

*Date* 1819

Fort William takes its name from a stone fort built at Inver-lochy under William II of Scotland (III of England) who reigned from 1689-1702. It replaced an earlier temporary structure erected by General Monck. Prior to the building of 'Fort' William the settlement was known as Maryburgh. The fort was one of several government fortifications along the line of the Great Glen, others being at Fort Augustus and Inverness. Permanently garrisoned during the late seventeenth and early eighteenth centuries, these forts were intended to assist in the pacification of the clans. The Gaelic name means simply 'The Garrison'.

Today Fort William is a small town on Loch Linnhe at the western end of the Caledonian Canal. It is popular with tourists and has a number of industries. The nearby mountains, domin-ated by Ben Nevis, provide both minerals and hydro-electric power and during the winter months ski-ing. The town is the home of the excellent West Highland Museum, which has many interesting exhibits relating to the history of the area. Fort William is linked by rail to Glasgow by the scenic West Highland Line, which extends westwards to Mallaig. This northern section is the route for nostalgic steam-powered express trains, which are very popular with tourists.

The Fort William district tartan was first included in Wilsons of Bannockburn, 1819 Pattern Book (p. 19).

| G | A | LG | A | bK | A | bK | G | bK | A | bK |
|----|----|----|----|----|----|----|----|----|----|----|
| 34 | 4 | 4 | 4 | 42 | 4 | 6 | 60 | 4 | 4 | 8 |

# GALA WATER

*Designer* Wilsons of Bannockburn

*Date* 1819

Gala Water, a south-flowing tributary of the Tweed, rises in a series of burns draining the Moorfoot Hills and Dun Law to the south of Edinburgh. The town of Galashiels stands on Gala Water just above its confluence with the Tweed. It capitalised on its position, in a land suitable for sheep raising, by the establishment of woollen mills powered by water, before electricity was available for this purpose. As a result the town became a major centre for Scotland's woollen industry, which has declined in recent years. Galashiels nevertheless, is still the home of one of Scotland's major manufacturers of tartan. The Scottish College of Textiles has also been established in the town and is devoted to research and training for careers in one of Scotland's most famous and important industries, the manufacture of textiles, particularly those made from wool.

The Gala Water district tartan, sometimes referred to as the 'Gallowater' was first recorded in the records of Wilsons of Bannockburn in 1793. It is included also in some Wilson manuscript notes (at present in the Royal Museum of Scotland) which date to about 1800 (*R*20 bK36 A20 B36 G80 *Y* 10). A second sett with slightly different proportions and the addition of white lines appears in the Wilsons 1819 Key Pattern Book. This is illustrated opposite and is often referred to as the 'new' sett. A third sett, commonly known as Gala Water 'old' omits both the red band and the white line. This also appears in Wilsons Key Pattern Book of 1819.

| **R** | bK | A | P | W | G | **Y** |
|-------|-----|-----|-----|-----|-----|-------|
| 10 | 32 | 14 | 32 | 2 | 42 | 10 |

# GALLOWAY

*Designer* John Hannay

*Date* 1950

Galloway is an ancient division of southwest Scotland, broadly co-extensive with the former counties of Wigtown and Kirk-cudbright. These counties, together with Dumfriesshire and parts of southern Ayrshire were absorbed into the Dumfries and Galloway Region in 1975. Galloway was to the early Gaelic speaker the land of the 'Gall' or 'foreigner', where the old Welsh-like British language was spoken. The name Galloway persisted as the Gaelic people came across from Ireland and replaced the earlier inhabitants. The Rinns of Galloway and the coast of Ulster are only 18 miles apart. The two areas shared a mutual language and culture for centuries and today are directly linked by a ferry service from Stranraer. Galloway is a pastoral land, still lonely and uncultivated in many areas. The 'Gallowa' Hills', often called the 'Galloway Highlands' are a favourite haunt for the visitor seeking beauty and solitude.

The Galloway district tartan was designed in 1950 by John Hannay, a chiropodist, living in London. In contemporary correspondence, Mr Hannay stated that the Galloway 'every-day' tartan was 'in four shades of green with yellow and red stripe' (sic). As woven on his behalf, however, by Cree Mills Ltd. of Newton-Stewart, Wigtownshire, only two shades of green were used, as indicated below. In some samples received by the Scottish Tartans Society, the yellow line has been replaced by a white one, possibly because it was originally intended to be a primrose shade.

Mr Hannay, at the same time designed the Galloway dress tartan. This is a colour change of the 'everyday' tartan together with a modification of the proportions of each colour in the sett.

Galloway is also a surname borne by a number of families, who sometimes choose to wear the Galloway tartans.

| *Everyday* | | | | | | | *Dress* | | | | | |
|---|---|---|---|---|---|---|---|---|---|---|---|---|
| **R** | DG | MossG | DG | MossG | **Y** | | **G** | R | B | R | B | **Y** |
| 6 | 4 | 64 | 64 | 4 | 6 | | 4 | 2 | 32 | 32 | 2 | 6 |

# GLASGOW

*Gaelic Name*

**Glaschu**

*Designer* Unknown

*Date* Pre 1819

Glasgow is perceived by many to be a product of the modern industrial age. In truth, St Mungo set up his church near the banks of the River Clyde more than fourteen hundred years ago. Parts of Glasgow Cathedral date from the 1200s and the university, founded in 1451, is Scotland's second oldest. The oldest house in Glasgow, Provand's Lordship, was built in 1471. The Mitchell Library is the largest public reference library in Europe.

Commercial cycles have brought prosperity followed by difficult times — the great tobacco 'boom', then textiles, then the industrial revolution fuelled by the coalpits of central Scotland. Clyde-built ships, such as the *Queen Mary*, set world standards, Glasgow is Scotland's largest urban centre, the hub of a ring of smaller industrial and commercial towns. Much of the central city dates from the early 1800s and the older sections have given way to new highrise office and apartment buildings and the busy motorways.

The Glasgow tartan dates from 1819. For several decades a weaving error gave rise to an alternative pattern. Research has restored the original pattern as shown in the illustration. The tartan is unique in that it specifies that the reddish colour be that of madder, one of the earliest red-producing dye plants. It is included in the 1819 Pattern Book of Wilsons of Bannockburn (p. 73).

| **P** | Madder | G | Madder | P | Madder | **G** |
|---|---|---|---|---|---|---|
| 4 | 8 | 50 | 42 | 48 | 8 | 50 |

# GLEN LYON

*Gaelic Name*

## Gleann Liobhunn

*Designer* Wilsons of Bannockburn

*Date* 1819

Glen Lyon, one of the longer glens of the Perthshire Highlands, opens onto the Tay Valley between Kenmore and Aberfeldy. The Roman camp at Fortingall near the foot of Glen Lyon attest to its long importance as an entrance to the Highlands.

The archives of the Scottish Tartans Society indicate that in the past there have been several versions of the Glen Lyon district tartan. These were investigated by some of the leading researchers of the Society, namely the late J. MacGregor Hastie, the late D.C. Stewart and James Scarlett, who prepared a report on the subject in 1965.

The first recorded reference to a Glen Lyon district tartan is in a letter, written in 1815, in the records of Wilsons of Bannockburn. No thread count is given but the firm's Key Pattern Book of 1819 (No. 53, p. 143) gives the sett as $A4$ $G8$ $bK10$. Other references, without thread counts, occur in 1826 and 1828. The late James McKinley noted a further sett ($A8$ bK8 $G7$) in an old Pattern Book believed to be from the firm of Gary and Dees of Perth. A slightly different count ($B8$ bK8 $G8$) is to be found in the Provist MacBean collection in Inverness.

A tartan sample pinned to a letter dated 26 September 1820 from Gloag Cochrane & Co. of Edinburgh to Wilsons is referred to in the order as Glen Lyon. It bears a strong resemblance to Wilsons Pattern No. 94 in which scarlet has been substituted for the azure of No. 53. Other variations occur.

The Glen Lyon district tartan as illustrated, is that which is accepted today. It was first noted by MacGregor Hastie but it is not certain how he obtained his sample. It has the same colours, azure, green and black as Wilsons Pattern No. 53 but in different proportions with black instead of green for one of the pivots. It is of interest that Wilsons Pattern No. 53 is now known by its alternative name, Mull, and has become the accepted district tartan for that island.

| A | bK | G |
|---|----|----|
| 8 | 8 | 12 |

# GLEN ORCHY

*Gaelic Name*

**Gleann Urchaidh**

*Designer* Wilsons of Bannockburn

*Date* Pre 1819

Glen Orchy is one of Argyll's loveliest glens. Cutting through the Western Grampians in a southwesterly direction from Bridge of Orchy, the River Orchy is joined by the River Lochy to pass along the Strath of Orchy, past Dalmally and onwards to Loch Awe. Though the glen is in Campbell country, the neighbouring Glen Strae was once the headquarters of the recalcitrant Clan MacGregor. Today Glen Orchy is a popular tourist route for those motorists who wish to avoid the arterial roads.

The sett illustrated is the now established Glen Orchy district tartan. It is taken from 'Old and Rare Scottish Tartans' by D. W. Stewart (1893) in which it is described as 'MacIntyre and Glenorchy'. It echoes the Glen Orchy sett in the 1819 Wilson's pattern book. (*G10* S8 Light pink 2 DB72 S8 G30 S16 LB2 DB30 S8 G72 S8 LP2 DB10 *LB2.*) It is possible that the sett may have evolved from the hand woven design procured from the Highlands by one of Wilson's agents. Two other setts named MacIntyre-Glenorchy are to be found in the records of the Highland Society of London (c.1820) No. 196 which is different in warp and weft and No. 473 (*A4* R6 G6 R10 B28 R6 G4 R10 B4 R6 G28 R10 B6 R6 *A4*).

| **G** | K | R | G | R | B | A | R | G | R | B | R | G | **K** |
|---|---|---|---|---|---|---|---|---|---|---|---|---|---|
| 4 | 4 | 6 | 36 | 6 | 12 | 2 | 8 | 12 | 4 | 36 | 6 | 4 | 4 |

# GLEN TILT

*Gaelic Name*

**Gleann Teilt**

*Designer* Clunes Farm, Blair Atholl

*Date* Pre 1923 (probably much older)

Glen Tilt cuts through the Grampian mountains of northern Perthshire. The River Tilt and its tributaries drain the eastern section of the wilderness of the Forest of Atholl, which, like many similarly named areas in Scotland, is a landscape devoid of trees. Woodland abounds, however, at the lower end of the glen where the waters of the River Tilt meet those of the River Garry near the village of Blair Atholl. The upper glen is one of Scotland's deepest glens and is renowned for its straightness. It is a lonely and remote spot, there being no public roads by which to reach it. Ancient tracks along the glen pass through the mountains near Loch Tilt to reach the Linn of Dee and Braemar.

The Glen Tilt district tartan is recorded as having been first woven at 'Clunes farm' which is probably the Clunes Lodge some six miles to the east of the southern entrance to the glen. The thread count given is taken from home-woven and home-dyed sample in the archives of Perth Museum (No. 2344). It has common elements with the Stewart of Urrard sett from nearby Killiecrankie. It provides an alternative sett for people wishing to associate themselves with the area.

| W | G | R | G | R | B | R | G | R | W |
|---|---|---|----|---|----|----|---|---|---|
| 4 | 4 | 4 | 56 | 4 | 24 | 44 | 4 | 4 | 4 |

# GLEN TROOL

*Date* Post 1945

Glen Trool is one of the most beautiful glens in southwest Scotland. It cleaves through the Galloway uplands some eight miles north of Newton Stewart in the former county of Kirkcudbright, now for administrative purposes, part of the Dumfries & Galloway Region.

Two of the highest mountains of southern Scotland, Merrick (2770 feet, 843 metres) to the north and Lamachan Hill (2350 feet) to the south send feeder burns down into the glen. The Glen Trool National Park, which covers some 130,000 acres, attracts many thousands of visitors every year; it is heavily forested and includes the lovely Loch Trool. Many of the visitors to the area are surprised to find that many acres of southern Scotland are more 'highland' in character than part of the eastern side of the Highland Region several hundred miles to the north.

The Glen Trool tartan began life as a 'trade check' and was first entered in the Register of All Publicly Known Tartans in this category. For the uninitiated a trade check is a tartan which was introduced as a colourful fashion fabric and given a name merely to identify it. This sett has proved to be very popular, however, and has now become fully established as a district tartan.

| **G** | T | G | R | **T** |
|-------|----|----|----|----|
| 74 | 18 | 6 | 18 | 6 |

# HUNTLY

*Gaelic Name*

**Hunndaigh**

*Designer* Unknown

*Date* Pre 1717

Huntly is a town in Strathbogie near the confluence of the Rivers Deveron and Bogie. The early parts of Huntly Castle, now a ruin, date from the twelfth century but it was largely built in the 1400s. This district was given to Sir Adam, Lord of Gordon, by Robert the Bruce for services rendered, and has remained part of the Gordon estates until this day. The Chief of Clan Gordon is the Marquis of Huntly who now resides at Aboyne. The present feudal Baron of Huntly is successor in title to a former Duke of Richmond, Gordon and Lennox. The complex Huntly tartan is perhaps one of the most authentic 'district' tartans known. It appears to have been in general use in about 1745 by members of several clans in this area — Gordon, Ross, Brodie, Forbes, Munro and MacRae. It was worn, with a slight variation, by Prince Charles Edward in 1745 while a guest of the MacRaes, one of whom is believed to have worn a version of the tartan at the Battle of Sherrifmuir in 1715. The tartan may have had a Jacobite identification. Today, it remains its district affiliation but is sometimes worn as an alternative sett by the clans mentioned above.

There are several variations of the Huntly District sett on record but the proportions given below are those stated by D. C. Stewart.

| G | R | G | R | G | R | G | R | W | R | Y | B | R | B | Y | R |   |
|----|----|----|----|----|----|----|----|----|----|----|----|----|----|----|----|----|
| 16 | 4 | 16 | 24 | 4 | 6 | 4 | 24 | 2 | 6 | 2 | 24 | 6 | 24 | 2 | 6 |   |
| W | R | B | R | B | R | B | R | B | R | B | R | B | R | G | R | G |
| 2 | 24 | 2 | 2 | 4 | 2 | 2 | 24 | 2 | 2 | 4 | 2 | 2 | 24 | 16 | 4 | 16 |

# INVERNESS

*Gaelic Name*

**Inbhir Nis**

*Designer* Unknown
*Date* Pre 1822

Inverness, the opening (inbhir) of the Ness, is the largest town in the north of Scotland and the administrative centre for the Highlands and Islands. It is the eastern terminus of the Great Glen, the natural rift through the Highlands that has provided a path for commerce and travel since man first came to Scotland. Columba came through the Great Glen to the capital of the heathen Picts to convert their king to Christianity. Columba reported the first documented sighting of the Loch Ness 'monster' at the foot of Loch Ness a short distance from the modern town. In the nineteenth century the Caledonian Canal made it possible to traverse Scotland by water. The railway south to Edinburgh and west to Kyle (for Skye) made Inverness the 'Capital of the Highlands'.

Today the modern town spans the River Ness. The Castle was re-built in the nineteenth century and the town has a fine museum. Tradition lives and Inverness is the home of 'The Northern Meeting', one of the oldest and most important of piping competitions.

The Inverness tartan was woven for Augustus, the Earl of Inverness (see also *Royal Tartans*, p. 15), sometime before 1822. It was the first tartan ever to be reproduced as a colour illustration in a book on tartans. Although sometimes called the 'Burgh of Inverness' tartan, Augustus' title of Earl (Count) makes the tartan appropriate to the whole county of Inverness. The illustration shows pale yellow substituted for white, as occasionally occurs.

| **R** | B | W | B | G | bK | G | **R** |
|---|---|---|---|---|---|---|---|
| 72 | 6 | 2 | 12 | 2 | 2 | 2 | 18 |

# LARGS

*Gaelic Name*

## Na Leargaidh Ghallda

*Designer* Sidney Samuels

*Date* 1981

Largs, a historic town on the Firth of Clyde, is today a favourite tourist resort. Families play on the sands of history. During the early Middle Ages the jurisdiction of the King of Scots was confined to the mainland, the islands being part of the Kingdom of Norway, and Kings Alexander I and II moved to bring the Western Isles under Scottish rule. In response, King Hakon of Norway brought a fleet to Scotland to maintain Norse sovereignty. The Norwegians landed at Largs in October 1263, and were defeated by the Scots. The peace treaty that followed made the Hebrides part of Scotland although the Outer Hebrides are still named in Gaelic *Innse Ghall* — the 'islands of the Foreigners', referring to the Norse. Orkney and Shetland remained part of Norway for several more centuries. The Gaelic name reminds Highlanders that there is another place by the same name. Modern Largs is 'the Lowland Largs'.

The Largs tartan is a new design, created for the town and officially adopted in 1981. There is also a 'dress' version.

| **RB** | R | DB | W | DB | T | DB | T | DB | T | RB | R | **W** |
|------|---|----|----|----|---|----|---|----|----|----|---|------|
| 4 | 4 | 44 | 6 | 5 | 4 | 3 | 8 | 3 | 16 | 4 | 22 | 4 |

# LENNOX

*Gaelic Name*
## Na Leainhanaich
*Designer* Unknown
*Date* Pre 1600

Lennox, once an extensive district to the north of Glasgow at the southernmost end of the Highlands, today centres around the village of Lennoxtown, the nearby state forest and Lennox Castle. The Lennox district tartan was taken from a copy of a sixteenth-century portrait of a lady supposed to be the countess of Lennox, mother of Henry Darnley, the second husband of Mary, Queen of Scots and father of James VI. Thus, the tartan is very old, one of the oldest recorded, dating from the second half of the 1500s. The tartan is unusual in that it combines two different shades of red or scarlet. The light green is often referred to as 'myrtle'.

Families with the surname 'Lennox' are usually considered related to Clans Stewart or MacFarlane. Some of this surname also choose to wear the distinctive and ancient 'Lennox' tartan.

| **LG** | W | LG | DR | LR | DR | **LR** |
|--------|---|----|----|----|----|--------|
| 4 | 2 | 20 | 4 | 20 | 2 | 4 |

# LOCHABER

*Gaelic Name*

**Loch Abair**

*Designer* Unknown

*Date* Pre 1800

Lochaber (probably meaning the loch of the confluence) is the home of Clan Cameron and a portion of the Clanranald MacDonalds. Here the Great Glen opens to the western sea at the foot of Ben Nevis, the highest mountain in the British Isles. Lochaber is a land almost surrounded by lochs — Loch Lochy, Loch Moy and Loch Treig to the north and east; 'Lochaber' itself is formed to the west and south where Loch Eil and Loch Leven flow into great Loch Linnhe, the long sea arm that stretches west to Mull, 'land's end'. Fort William, the population centre of Lochaber, was founded to secure and pacify the Western Highlands. It was the departure point to America for many Gaels, and one of the most touching of bagpipe laments is the beautiful slow march 'Lochaber No More'.

The town has its own beautiful tartan (see p. 68). There are several recorded authentic old patterns from the 'Lochaber' district. The sett given below is taken from the Wilson Key Pattern book of 1819.

| G | A | B | R | bK | G | bK | R | bK | G |
|---|---|----|---|----|----|----|---|----|---|
| 8 | 4 | 66 | 4 | 70 | 66 | 2 | 4 | 2 | 8 |

# LOCH LAGGAN

*Gaelic Name*

**Loch Lagan**

*Designer* Unknown

*Date* pre 1820

Loch Laggan is a lovely loch on the historic route between Lochaber and the Great Glen and the Central Highlands of Badenoch. Separated from the headwaters of the River Spey by a low divide, Loch Laggan is a partially forested loch at the head of Glen Spean, draining into its smaller companion, Loch Moy. From here the River Spean drops westward into the Great Glen to join the River Lochy.

The Loch Laggan tartan is appropriate for those who know and love Glen Spean. The earliest known record of this tartan is in the collection of the Highland Society of London. The specimen there has the warp woven at 82 threads to the inch and the weft at 75 threads to the inch. As a result the proportions in each are slightly different. The count given below is that of the warp.

| **G** | bK | G | R | G | **R** |
|-------|-----|-----|-----|-----|-------|
| 14 | 14 | 202 | 14 | 12 | 38 |

# LOCH RANNOCH

*Gaelic Name*

**Loch Rannaich**

*Designer* Mrs P. J. Thompson

*Date* 1975

Loch Rannoch — 'It's by Tummel, and Loch Rannoch, and Lochaber I will go' promise the words to the spirited song 'The Road to the Isles'. From time immemorial, the traditional route from the Lothians and Fife to the West was across Perthshire by way of the Tay, the River Tummel, along Loch Rannoch and across Rannoch Moor to the glens of Lochaber. Early Bronze Age hunters skirted Ben Nevis to reach the sea through Glen Nevis and Glencoe. Later their trails were followed by cattle drovers and, at times, the royal armies of clansmen, princes and kings. Robert Louis Stevenson set the escape of David Balfour and Alan Breck in the book *Kidnapped* across Rannoch Moor. In later years it became the route of the West Highland Railway. Today Loch Rannoch is a favourite vacation spot known for its beauty in both winter and summer. It is no longer on a major highway and the visitor can escape the pace of modern urban life.

The Loch Rannoch tartan is a good example of a fashion 'trade check' which has become accepted as a district tartan by the area which gave it its name. It was designed by Mrs P. J. Thompson (Clan Crest Textiles Ltd) in 1975.

| **DT** | G | DT | LT | G | LT | Buff | **DT** |
|--------|---|----|----|---|----|------|--------|
| 48 | 4 | 10 | 28 | 4 | 10 | 34 | 4 |

# LORNE

*Gaelic Name*
**Lathurna**
*Designer* Mr Ross (from Glasgow)
*Date* 1871

Lorn is rolling fertile land to the southeast of the Firth of Lorn, separated from the rest of Argyll by the natural barrier of Loch Awe. Oban is the major population and cultural centre. A fishing port, it is also the terminus of the ferries to most of the more southerly of the Western Isles. The Oban 'Gold Medal' is one of the premier bagpipe competitions. The interior of Lorn is good country for cattle and sheep and its many streams and rivers provide fine salmon fishing.

Lorn is the country of Clan Campbell and the son of the Duke of Argyll is styled the Marquess of Lorne. The Lorne tartan was designed in 1871 to commemorate the marriage of the Marquess (John, later 9th Duke) to Princess Louise, daughter of Queen Victoria. It is a simple design but of striking beauty, incorporating the same colours as the tartan of Clan Campbell. Today, the Lorne is considered appropriate for residents or visitors to the district with no clan or family tartan of their own.

The sett given below appeared in W. & A. K. Johnston's *The tartans of the Clans and Septs of Scotland*, 1906.

| **B** | bK | G | bK | G | bK | G | bK | B | bK | B | bK | B | bK | **G** |
|---|---|---|---|---|---|---|---|---|---|---|---|---|---|---|
| 8 | 4 | 32 | 4 | 4 | 4 | 4 | 32 | 4 | 4 | 4 | 4 | 32 | 4 | 8 |

# MAR

*Gaelic Name*
## A 'Mharr

*Designer* Unknown

*Date* Early twentieth century but possibly older

The traditional pipe march 'The Standard on the Braes of Mar' celebrates the opening of the Jacobite Rising in 1715. Mar is the high ground between the upper reaches of the Rivers Dee and Don. Here, on the gentle slopes or 'braes' man has long found fertile ground and natural highways from the coast to the eastern Highlands. Queen Victoria and Prince Albert built their Scottish home at Balmoral, still a favourite residence of the Royal Family. Today 'Braigh Mharr' is a major attraction for visitors and a centre for the preservation of Scottish culture through the Highland Games at Aboyne, Ballater and Braemar.

There is uncertainty with regard to the origin of the simple but striking 'Mar District' tartan. In the seventh edition of Frank Adam's *Clan Septs and Regiments*, it is stated that the sett was obtained under the name Skene 'from the Duke of Fife' (whose ancestors owned Mar Lodge). A more complex sett is given for the family of Skene. Because the Skenes lived in the Mar district and were known as Clan Donnachaidh Mhairr (the Robertsons of Mar) the connection between the two names is apparent. Indeed, the Mar district tartan could have evolved either by a misreading or by intent from the Skene sett depicted on the apron of the Skene kilt illustrated by R. R. McIan in the *Clans of the Scottish Highlands* (1845 & 47). The Skene sett is stated to have been taken from an old kilt preserved in the Castle of Skene. On the other hand, the Mar District sett may have been a simple design extant before 1845 upon which the more elaborate Clan Skene tartan was based.

A variant of the sett of Mar District tartan given below was recorded in 1978 in the Books of the Court of the Lord Lyon (Writs section) pursuant to a petition by the Rt. Hon. Margaret of Mar, Countess of Mar so that it might be 'known and recognised as the proper tartan of the Tribe of Mar'.

| **R** | bK | G | bK | **Y** |
|-------|----|----|----|-------|
| 2 | 3 | 45 | 3 | 2 |

# MENTEITH

*Gaelic Name*
## Teadhaich
*Designer* Unknown
*Date* Probably post 1831

Menteith lies between the waters of the River Teith and the upper reaches of the River Forth. The Lake of Menteith is Scotland's only body of water referred to as a 'lake' — all other Scottish lakes are called 'lochs'. The district has always been agricultural and remains so to this day. The Menteith Hills lie between Aberfoyle and Callander, on the edge of the Trossachs, some of Scotland's most spectacular scenery.

Menteith gave its name to the western branch of the Graham family. The 'Menteith District' tartan was formerly known as the District Stewartry of Menteith. It is similar in colour to that of 'Graham of Menteith' which was first recorded in Logan's *The Scottish Gael* in 1831 (*G32* A4 G2 bK24 B24 *bK2*). The proportions of colours are quite distinct, however, and the azure stripe in the family tartan is replaced by white in the district. The Menteith District tartan was rescued from oblivion in 1941 by Graeme Menteith who wrote to MacGregor Hastie about it.

| **G** | W | G | bK | B | **bK** |
|-------|---|----|----|----|-------|
| 18 | 2 | 12 | 14 | 14 | 2 |

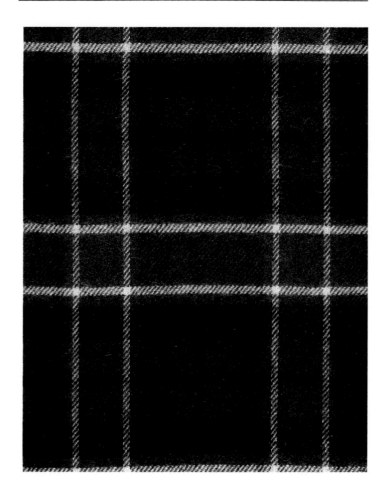

# MOFFAT

*Designer* Unknown

*Date* Possibly 1920-1940

Moffat Water, rising on the steep hills of Dumfriesshire, runs in almost a straight south-west line to the River Annan. Three miles above the juncture is the small resort town of Moffat, just off the main Glasgow to Carlisle road. The Moffat district was for centuries, part of the domain of the Douglases and later, of the Johnstons who resided a short way southwest of the present village at Lochwood.

Moffat today is one of the loveliest villages of Scotland with a large central square lined with shops and hotels. Just beyond the village, one can find straths, glens and mountains that rival the best of Highland scenery. This traditional pastoral land is filled with songs and stories of early cattle drovers and reivers. Just above Moffat, is the 'Devil's Beef Tub', a natural cul-de-sac which was traditionally the holding place for stolen cattle. Some miles to the south is the birthplace of King Robert the Bruce at Lochmaben.

The origin of the Moffat district tartan is unclear. It was possibly designed as a family tartan during the interwar years in the first half of this century. It was first noted by John MacGregor Hastie and seems to be based on the centre portion of the Murray of Tullibardine sett, though in somewhat different proportions of the red and green. When Major Francis Moffat of that Ilk M.C. was recognised as Chief of the Name and House of Moffat, by the Lord Lyon in 1983 (after the family had been without a chief for 420 years), a family tartan of different design and based on the Douglas was introduced to commemorate early family connections.

| bK | R | B | R | G | R | B | R | B | R |
|----|----|----|----|----|----|----|----|----|-----|
| 2 | 4 | 4 | 16 | 32 | 24 | 2 | 2 | 32 | 128 |

# MULL

*Gaelic Name*
## Muile

*Designer* Wilsons of Bannockburn

*Date* 1819

Mull, *Muile* — 'Land's End' — is one of the largest and most populous islands of the Inner Hebrides. It is the guardian of the entrance to Loch Linnhe and the Great Glen through the Firth of Lorn, dominated by the MacLean Castle of Duart on Mull. Mull is a mountainous island, Beinn Mhor rising to 3,169 feet (966 metres) within two miles of the sea. Iona, off the Ross of Mull, is the most sacred place in Scottish Gaeldom. Here Columba and his Irish missionaries landed to bring Christianity to the north of Scotland. Generations of Scottish kings lie buried on Iona. Today the rebuilt cathedral there is a place of pilgrimage for both Scots and visitors. Tobermory Bay (*Tobar Mhoire* —Mary's Well) is known for the Spanish galleon with its supposed treasure that sank there after the defeat of the Armada in 1588.

There are probably more well-known Gaelic songs about Mull and by natives of Mull than any other place in Scotland. It is a rare Gaelic concert that will not include *An t-Eilean Muileach* or *Muile nam Fuar Bheann Ard* ('Mull of the Cold High Mountains'). Easily visible from Oban, the island is well worth the short crossing.

The Mull tartan is one of the simplest of the district setts. It was first recorded by Wilsons of Bannockburn and is also listed by their company as No. 53 or Glen Lyon (for which there is another distinctive sett described elsewhere in this book).

| A | G | bK |
|---|---|----|
| 4 | 8 | 10 |

# MUSSELBURGH

*Designer* G. Lawson

*Date* 1958

Musselburgh, a burgh on the Firth of Forth, at the mouth of the River Esk, dates from medieval times. Its Tolbooth dates from the sixteenth century. A centre of fishing and marketing for the rich lands of Midlothian, the town clearly was first famous for the harvesting of mussels on the banks of the Forth. Musselburgh saw the establishment of the first machine-made fishing net industry in the 1820s and coalmining was an important industry southwest of the town. As Edinburgh, only six miles away, has grown over the past two centuries, Musselburgh has become part of the greater urban complex that now surrounds the capital ciy. Nevertheless, Musselburgh retains its own personality, identity and pride.

The Musselburgh District tartan was designed for the town celebrations of 1958-59 by G. Lawson of the Musselburgh Co-operative Society. Since then it has become very popular. Its design and colours make it suitable for ready-to-wear skirts, the purchasers of which are often unaware of its territorial connections.

| **A** | W | A | Y | A | W | A | B | **R** |
|----|---|---|---|---|---|---|----|---|
| 28 | 2 | 6 | 4 | 6 | 2 | 8 | 48 | 6 |

# NITHSDALE

*Gaelic Name*
**Srath Nid**
*Designer* Arthur Galt
*Date* 1930

Nithsdale, the valley of the River Nith, stretches over fifty miles, north to south, through the length of Dumfriesshire to the sea. It takes its name from a mixture of Brythonic and Scottish words, meaning 'valley of the new river'. Perhaps no other area is as famous in Scottish music as this one. Burns immortalised the small tributary of Afton Water and Maxwelltown's Braes were home to 'Annie Laurie'.

The River Nith, which abounds in salmon, was early harnessed to bring industry to Dumfries, the only major town in the area. Nithsdale is rich in history. It was the territory of the Maxwells who controlled the region from their stronghold at Caerlaverock on the eastern side of the Nith estuary. This castle, now in ruins, was Sir Walter Scott's 'Ellangowan'. On the other side of the estuary, formerly crossed by the old thirteenth century town bridge in Dumfries, now reserved for foot traffic, lies New Abbey. Perhaps better known as 'Sweetheart Abbey', it was founded in 1273 by Devorguilla, in memory of her husband John Balliol, founder, along with her, of Balliol College, Oxford. Their son, John Balliol (1249-1313), was King of Scots.

The Nithsdale tartan is appropriate for both residents and the many visitors to the area and, with the 'Galloway' tartans, could well serve as a tartan representative of Dumfries and the surrounding region. It uses only three colours, blue, red and green, to form a very pleasing sett. It was designed by Arthur Galt of Messrs. Hugh Galt and Sons Ltd., Barrhill, Ayrshire in cooperation with Councillor John Hannay.

| **B** | R | G | R | G | R | G | R | G | **R** |
|-------|---|---|---|----|----|---|---|---|----|
| 20 | 4 | 4 | 12 | 32 | 2 | 4 | 2 | 6 | 12 |

# PAISLEY

*Gaelic Name*

**Paislig**

*Designer* Allan C. Drennan

*Date* 1952

Paisley, a manufacturing centre only seven miles from Glasgow, is more famous for its shawls than for tartan. Paisley began as a village around a monastery founded in 1163 by Walter Fitzallan, progenitor of the royal line of the Stewart family. In 1488 it became a burgh. Nearby, is Elderslie, the traditional birthplace of William Wallace. King Robert III was buried in Paisley Abbey in 1406.

The name comes ultimately from Latin *Basilica* a church, possibly through an old Welsh form.

The town became a textile centre specialising in linen and silk-gauze in the early 1700s. In 1812, the production of cotton thread began and Paisley became one of the world's leading thread-manufacturing centres. The original Paisley shawls, inspired by contact with India, are now collector's items. Alexander Wilson, famed early American ornithologist, was a son of Paisley.

The attractive Paisley tartan was designed by Allan C. Drennan, who was the sub-manager of the Sporting Department of Anchor Mills, Paisley in 1952, when it won him first prize in its class at the Kelso Highland Show. He regarded it as having 'a motif of the Clan Donald'. Though created as a district tartan, the Paisley sett has been adopted by many people bearing that name, and by the Paisley & Allied Families Society, which regards it as a means of 'generating a family identity'.

| B | W | G | B | Y | bK | Y | G | R | G | R | G |
|----|---|---|----|---|----|---|----|----|---|---|----|
| 14 | 4 | 6 | 36 | 4 | 30 | 4 | 34 | 10 | 6 | 4 | 14 |

# PERTHSHIRE

*Gaelic Name*

## Siorramachd Pheairt

*Designer* Wilsons of Bannockburn

*Date* Pre 1831

Perthshire, the central shire at the 'waist' of Scotland, is the inland gateway to the Highlands. The casual driver, travelling along the main roads, misses the small glens and villages. Castles, ruined, restored and occupied, attract visitors. The 'Sma' Glen and Glen Almond are among the most picturesque in Scotland.

The Black Watch held their first muster in Perthshire and the Royalists won a short-lived victory at Killiecrankie. Jacobite plotters met secretly at Amulree. The New Testament was translated into Gaelic by James Stewart, Minister at Killin.

Perth, an ancient settlement, was a frequent royal residence until James I was murdered there in 1437. Built at the lowest navigable point on the Tay, the only corridor into the Highlands below the Dee, Perth was ideally sited to control Strathtay, the starting place for the Breadalbane route to Argyll and the Tummel route to Lochaber, the great Glen and the Hebrides. At the same time it controlled north-south communications along Strath Allan from Stirling through Strathearn and Strathmore to the glens of Angus.

It was at Scone, just outside Perth, that the Kings of Scots were inaugurated on the stone that is still used in Royal coronations in Westminster Abbey. Scone Palace, built between 1803 and 1808, is open to the public.

The Perthshire tartan is a variation of a Drummond sett. The first record of this tartan is in the early nineteenth-century Account Book of Wilsons of Bannockburn when it is referred to as the 'Perthshire Rock and Wheel' being an early type of soft tartan. (*R*82 W4 P10 Y4 G42 R18 P10 DB6 *W*4). The sett woven today is of slightly differing proportions and is given below. There are also a number of dress versions of this tartan.

| **R** | W | B | Y | G | R | B | A | **W** |
|---|---|---|---|---|---|---|---|---|
| 72 | 2 | 6 | 2 | 32 | 16 | 6 | 4 | 2 |

# ROTHESAY

*Gaelic Name*

## Baile Bhoid

*Designer* Vestiarium Scoticum

*Date* Pre 1842

Rothesay is the principal town of the Island of Bute, in the Firth of Clyde. Bute is a low rolling island, cultivated for centuries and is home to the Stuarts of Bute, a major branch of Clan Stewart and their dependents, the MacKirdys/MacCurdys. Part of the island was for many years the *duthchas* of the Fulltertons and, later, the property of the Boyds, whose name may come from the Gaelic name for the island.

In the last century, Rothesay and Rothesay Bay became popular holiday spots, a popularity remembered in song which continues until the present. A haven for pleasure boats, the island is linked to the mainland by ferry from Wemyss Bay.

Rothesay is also a historic royal burgh, from which derives the title of Duke of Rothesay, held by the sovereign's eldest son since 1469. The Rothesay tartan, previously unknown, appeared in the *Vestiarium Scoticum* in 1842 under the name of 'the Prince of Rothesay'. It is based on early forms of the Royal Stewart sett. It was worn by the later King Edward VII as a small child in 1844, when he was Duke of Rothesay and Prince of Wales.

There is a hunting version in W. & A. K. Johnston's *The Tartans of the Clans and Septs of Scotland*, 1906 (G8 R32 G8 R4 G6 R4 G64 W2 G2 W4).

| **W** | R | W | R | G | R | G | R | G | R | G | R |
|----|----|----|----|----|----|----|----|----|----|----|----|
| 4 | 2 | 2 | 64 | 4 | 6 | 4 | 8 | 32 | 8 | 32 | 8 | 4 | 6 |

| G | R | **W** |
|----|----|----|
| 4 | 64 | 4 |

# ROXBURGH

*Designer* Unknown

*Date* Pre 1850

Roxburgh, the county of the Middle March, is among the most beautiful and historic areas of Scotland. Now included in the administrative region known as the 'Borders', Roxburgh is the true Border county. Here the Roman armies came and withdrew to build Hadrian's Wall to restrain the warlike Scots. Crusaders, Kings, Queens and the great Border Clans made this land along the River Teviot rich in history, tradition and spirit.

There are two recorded Roxburgh tartans. A red sett labelled 'Roxburgh' is taken from a silk in Patterson's Sample Book in the Scottish Tartans Society's library. A green pattern, a variation of a Douglas tartan, was recorded by Dr Philip Smith in 1952 from a piece of tartan labelled 'Roxburgh' dating from the period between the two World Wars. The red Roxburgh, now woven commercially for the first time in perhaps a century and a half, is gaining recognition as a truly representative district tartan.

|  | | | | *Green* | | | | |
|---|---|---|---|---|---|---|---|---|
| **B** | R | G | B | W | B | W | **B** | |
| 6 | 2 | 44 | 16 | 2 | 2 | 2 | 46 | |

|  | | | | *Red* | | | | | |
|---|---|---|---|---|---|---|---|---|---|
| **B** | DG | B | R | B | R | B | R | DG | **W** |
| 6 | 52 | 6 | 6 | 40 | 6 | 6 | 52 | 10 | 6 |

# ST ANDREWS

*Gaelic Name*

## Cill Rimhinn

*Designer* A. A. Bottomley

*Date* 1930

St Andrews is the home of two great Scottish institutions, the world famous university founded in 1411 and the Scottish national game, golf. Located on the tip of Fife, the famous 'Old Course', the mecca of golfers worldwide, lies at one end of the town while the ruins of the great Cathedral stand at the other. St Andrews is a favourite holiday town for tourists both from Scotland and from abroad.

The Earl of St Andrews tartan was created in 1930 by Mr A. A. Bottomley, a respected designer of tartans, for the personal use of Prince George, who bore this Scottish title. The Prince, who is probably remembered more readily as the late Duke of Kent, wore it in London at a dinner of the Highland Society in 1939, three years before he was killed on active service during the Second World War. His daughter, Princess Alexandra of Kent (the Hon. Mrs Angus Ogilvy) also wore it as a family tartan in the 1950s.

Since then it has progressively become accepted as a district tartan for the town of St Andrews where it is sold in a variety of garments and accessories. It is a simple and attractive design, reflecting the white and blue traditionally associated with the Saltire, the cross of St Andrew. It may be regarded as a compliment to the present Earl of St Andrews, George, the elder son of the now Duke of Kent, that his grandfather's tartan is now proudly worn by people all over the world, especially by those having connections with the town of St Andrews.

| LRB | LNB | W | LNB | W | LNB |
|-----|-----|-----|-----|-----|-----|
| 104 | 56 | 10 | 6 | 4 | 20 |

# STIRLING AND BANNOCKBURN

*Gaelic Name*

**Sruighlea**

*Designer* Wilsons of Bannockburn

*Date* c.1847

Stirling and Bannockburn are at the heart of Scottish history. Rugged mountains to the west and the broad Firth of Forth to the east effectively pinch Scotland into two parts; north and south, Highlands and Lowlands. Until modern times, only the fords and later the bridge at Stirling, provided practical land access between the two halves of Scotland and these were controlled by the great fortress of Stirling Castle. Defeat of the English by William Wallace at Stirling Bridge in 1297 and by Robert the Bruce at nearby Bannockburn seventeen years later, preserved Scottish independence.

The Stirling and Bannockburn tartan pattern was woven by the noted firm of Wilsons of Bannockburn and appears in Book IV of their records. It was used at the time by the Stirling and Bannockburn Caledonian Society. First rewoven by John Cargill of Dundee, an expert on tartan, it has regained popularity as an authentic old tartan woven almost a century and a half ago by a firm located in the very district after which the tartan was named.

| R | G | R | A | R | bK | R | B | G | Y |
|---|---|---|---|---|----|---|---|---|---|
| 6 | 36 | 8 | 6 | 8 | 26 | 6 | 36 | 4 | 6 |

# STRATHCLYDE

*Gaelic Name*

**Srath Chluaidh**

*Designer* Laird-Portch of Scotland

*Date* 1975

Strathclyde, the broad drainage of the River Clyde, was an independent Kingdom of Britons — speakers of a language akin to Welsh — until the eleventh century. It had its capital at Dumbarton ('fort of the Britons'), on the north bank of the river, but most of its territory was to the south, in what is now southwest Scotland. In 1975, this ancient name was given to the largest of Scotland's new Regions; it stretches from the former Ayrshire in the south, across the west central industrial belt, and includes part of Argyll and some of the more southerly of the Western Isles. Glasgow is the major city of both Strathclyde and Scotland, and is the home of Strathclyde University.

The Strathclyde tartan is one of the more recent designs and is appropriate for persons living in the historic river valley south of Glasgow and its immediate suburbs — Monklands, Eastwood, East Kilbride, Hamilton, Motherwell and Lanark. The tartan was designed in 1975 to fulfil a need for a tartan representative of the area. The navy blue and white are said to represent the 'Scottish sporting colours'.

| bK | A | W | NB | W | bK | W |
|----|----|----|----|----|----|----|
| 4 | 32 | 4 | 32 | 30 | 4 | 4 |

# STRATHEARN

*Gaelic Name*

**Srath Eireann**

*Designer* Unknown

*Date* Pre 1820

Strathearn, the beautiful and rich valley of the River Earn, lies between the front range of the Ochil Hills and the steep front of the Highland massif. The word *earn* means 'back part' or 'stern' in Gaelic and may be well chosen. Along the Earn, running parallel to the foot of the Highlands from Loch Earn to the Firth of Tay, are the sites of Roman army camps and outposts that mark the limit of the Roman frontier of the Empire — the 'outback' of Rome. St Fillans, at the eastern end of Loch Earn, commemorates the early missionary who brought Christianity to the region and from St Fillans, James MacGregor emigrated to become the Gaelic-speaking minister to the Scottish settlement at Pictou, Nova Scotia.

Monuments, famous names and historic spots abound in Strathearn, the home of generations of Scottish soldiers and statesmen. Perhaps the best known is Henry Dundas, Viscount Melville, whose monument above Comrie can be seen for miles. Drummond Castle, with its gardens and the famous Gleneagles Hotel and golf courses, bring many visitors. The Scottish Tartans Museum is located in the former weaving village of Comrie.

The Strathearn tartan is said to have been worn by the father of Queen Victoria, H.R.H. Edward, Duke of Kent, who was also Earl of Strathearn.

| Y | R | G | R | G | Y | G | R | Y | R | G | R | Y | G | R | Y |
|---|---|---|---|---|---|---|---|---|---|---|---|---|---|---|---|
| 2 | 2 | 12 | 12 | 2 | 2 | 2 | 12 | 16 | 2 | 2 | 2 | 16 | 12 | 2 | 2 |

# STRATHSPEY

*Gaelic Name*
**Srath Spe**
*Designer* Unknown
*Date* c.1793

Strathspey, the village of the River Spey, is one of the loveliest and the most fertile areas of the Highlands. Rising in a tiny loch, the Spey flows east through the grassland of Badenoch to Kingussie (*Cinn a'Ghiuthsaich* — head of the fir forest). Here Strathspey proper begins at the Forest of Rothiemurchus, one of the last original forests of Britain. Strathspey is a major producer of malt whisky and the Spey, flowing directly to the sea with no major falls, is famous for its salmon fishing.

From Craigellachie, the cliff above Aviemore to Craigellachie, the village twenty-five miles down river, Strathspey was the home of Clan Grant. Grantown-on-Spey was planned in 1776 by Sir James Grant of Grant (whose family, after 1811, acquired the title of Earl of Seafield). Parts of Castle Grant date from the 1400s but most of the structure was built in the 19th century.

The Strathspey tartan is taken from the back of a waistcoat supposedly worn by an officer of the Strathspey Fencibles Regiment which was raised by General James Grant of Ballindalloch (1793-1799). The waistcoat was exhibited at the Highland Exhibition in Inverness in 1930, having been lent by Col. J. Grant Smith of Grantown-on-Spey. Instead of the number of black lines being two or four respectively on alternate blue squares, there are three on every such square.

In 1984, the Strathspey district tartan was recommended to the Royal Scottish Country Dance Society as being suitable for wear by dancers with no clear affiliation of their own.

| **bK** | B | bK | B | bK | G | **bK** |
|--------|---|----|----|----|----|--------|
| 4 | 4 | 4 | 20 | 20 | 20 | 4 |

# SUTHERLAND

*Gaelic Name*

**Cataibh**

*Designer* Unknown

*Date* Early eighteenth-century origin

Sutherland, though reaching to the northernmost coast of mainland Scotland, is the 'south land' from the perspective of Norway, Orkney and Caithness — lands under Norse rule. Much of this barren region is a 'wet' desert, flat plains with low sub-arctic vegetation and high, barren rocky mountains. Only along the coasts and in sheltered glens could man settle, living a hunting, fishing and small farming life from prehistory until a century ago. Many of the local population suffered greatly from their sudden removal during the 'Clearances' that thrust them unprepared into a rapidly industrialising nineteenth century.

The Sutherland tartan is of early eighteenth century origin and is distinct from the Clan Sutherland tartan. It has the same sett as the Government tartan, as worn by the Royal Highland Regiment (The Black Watch). It is traditionally woven in lighter shades, however, azure replacing the dark blue of the government pattern. It is worn by the Princess Louise's Argyll and Sutherland Highlanders, which regiment was formed in 1881 when the 93rd Sutherland Regiment was combined with the 91st Argyllshire Regiment. When worn by the military, the Sutherland tartan is usually worn kilted to the green in contrast to the darker Black Watch which is usually kilted to the blue.

The Sutherland sett is now firmly established as a district tartan for the county of Sutherland.

| **B** | bK | B | bK | B | bK | G | bK | G | bK | B | bK | **B** |
|---|---|---|---|---|---|---|---|---|---|---|---|---|
| 22 | 2 | 2 | 2 | 2 | 16 | 16 | 2 | 16 | 16 | 16 | 2 | 2 |

# TWEEDSIDE

*Designer* Wilsons of Bannockburn

*Date* c.1840

Tweedside indicates the drainage of the River Tweed, the
largest watershed of Scotland. Rising at Tweed's Well near
Moffat, the river runs through Peebles, Melrose and Kelso.
From Carham, the Tweed forms the border between Scotland
and England until it veers south to reach the sea at Berwick-
on-Tweed on the English side (see p. 136). The traditional
counties of this area are today known collectively as 'The
Borders' and this name was given in 1975 to one of Scotland's
new Regions. Robert the Bruce lies buried in the ruins of
Melrose Abbey while the monumental remains of Jedburgh and
ruined strongholds remind one of the vicious Border raids. This
is the land of the 'Border Clans' and of the constant struggle
with England for Scottish independence. In an area dominated
by several large feudal families, but with a large number of
surnames, the Tweedside tartan is appropriate for families and
friends of Tweeddale, Ettrick, Lauderdale and Berwickshire —
lands rich in history and tradition. The Tweedside tartan was
one of the patterns named after districts by Wilsons of Bannockburn. It appears in their Pattern Book No. 4 of c.1840 and
also in their scales of c.1847.

| bK | R/W | bK | R | W | R | W | R | bK |
|----|-----|----|---|---|---|---|---|----|
| 36 | 4 | 4 | 10 | 4 | 4 | 4 | 4 | 4 |

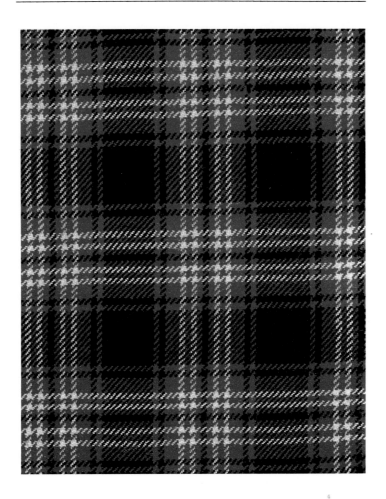

# SECTION III

# DISTRICT TARTANS OF THE BRITISH ISLES OUTWITH SCOTLAND

## CONTENTS

**ENGLAND**

Berwick-upon-Tweed 136
Cornwall
  (Cornish National) 138
Cornwall
  (Cornish Flag) 140
Cornwall
  (Cornish Hunting) 142
Cornwall
  (St Piran Dress) 144
Devon 146
Devon Companion 148
Durham 150
Somerset 152
Tyneside 154

**ISLE OF MAN**

Manx National 156
Isle of Man 158
Isle of Man
  (Laxey Manx) 160
Snaefell 162
Manx Hunting 164
Laxey (Centenary) 166

**IRELAND**

Clodagh 168
Tara 170
Ulster 172

**WALES**

Welsh National 174

# BERWICK-UPON-TWEED

*Designer* Alison Wilkinson

*Date* March 1982

Berwick-upon-Tweed is England's most northerly town being situated in Northumberland on the north bank of the River Tweed. Prior to the Union of the Crowns of England and Scotland in 1603, Berwick was the site of many skirmishes between the two countries. Indeed, between 1147 and 1482 it changed hands thirteen times. Today the town still has a distinct 'border town' atmosphere, for example, in the number of Scottish banks there. To commemorate the historic past of the town therefore, in 1981, the firm of Trow Mill (now closed) from Hawick, Scotland, arranged for its then Berwick branch, Marygate Weavers, to organise a competition for the design of a Berwick-upon-Tweed tartan. A number of designs were submitted by local people. In March 1982, the winner was announced, Alison Wilkinson of Wooler, Northumberland. She was at that time a pupil in form 3M of Berwick High School and received a prize of £50.

The black, red and gold of the tartan are the heraldic colours of the town and represent its corporate identity and the grey its many stone buildings. The blue symbolises the river Tweed and the green the nearby hills.

The tartan was woven and displayed at the town's quincentennial celebrations which began in August 1982 and at which the Royal Guest of Honour in the following month was the Duke of Gloucester. When first designed, it was woven as an asymmetric tartan, as illustrated, in which the half sett was repeated, rather than reversed. More recently it has been woven symmetrically with a half sett reverse.

| A | R | bK | G | bK | G | bK | N | O | G | O | G | O | R ... |
|---|---|----|---|----|---|----|---|---|---|---|---|---|-------|
| 8 | 16 | 10 | 4 | 8 | 4 | 10 | 76 | 10 | 4 | 8 | 4 | 10 | 18 |

# CORNWALL
# (CORNISH NATIONAL)

*Designer* E. E. Morton–Nance
(GWAS CWETHNOK)

*Date* 1963

Cornwall, the extremity of the south-west peninsula of the mainland of Britain, is regarded by many of its people as distinct from England as Scotland or Wales. Certainly, until conquered by the English king Athelstan in 936, it had enjoyed a virtually separate existence. Its essentially Celtic history still serves as an inspiration to many of its inhabitants and the ancient Cornish language, though no longer an everyday means of communication, has been revived by devotees. When certain Cornish patriots first decided to symbolise their Celtic origins by wearing the kilt, they chose plain black material with black stockings to match. This sombre dress had its critics and today, for example, the men of the traditional Cornish dance group, Cam Kernewek, may be seen wearing Cornish national tartan kilts, with black shirts and the women plaids over black skirts.

The Cornish tartan was the inspiration of a Cornish bard, Mr E. E. Morton-Nance, who regarded tartan as the heritage of all Celts, not Scots alone. He describes its symbolism in a poem written in Cornish entitled 'An Brythen Kernewek' the translation of which reads —

> From Celtic Cornwall's Tartan bright
> Shines Piran's Cross all blazing white
> — On Nation's Flag we bear it!
>
> The kilt of black and saffron swings;
> Tints blazoned by her ancient Kings
> — Brave Cornishmen, we wear it!
>
> O'er Blue Atlantic breakers rough
> Soars — crimson beaked — the sable chough
> — Embodied Arthur's Spirit . . .

The tartan has become very popular and has contributed to the uniting of Cornish people throughout the world.

| R | bK | A | Y | bK | W |
|---|----|---|---|----|---|
| 6 | 6 | 14 | 52 | 52 | 10 |

# CORNWALL (CORNISH FLAG)

*Designer* Ms Abi Armstrong Evans

*Date* 1983

The story of the tartans of Cornwall in many ways resembles that of those in the Isle of Man. The success of the Cornish national tartan was such that it prompted the introduction of further setts by different designers. One of these was Ms Abi Armstrong Evans who conceived the Cornish Flag tartan. She took her inspiration from the black and white cross of St Piran, which is linked with the Cornish flag and the Cornish national tartan. Black is also the colour of the Cornish Chough, the national bird of Cornwall along with red, the third shade in the tartan. The design was brought out in response to a demand for an alternative tartan to the Cornish national tartan, which would exclude the predominently yellow colouring, whist retaining a truly Cornish character. The Cornish Flag tartan, when first introduced, was known as the St Piran tartan and was to have been marketed in conjunction with Mr Donald Rawe of Padstow. Subsequently, there was a disagreement between the two parties and each decided to go their separate ways. Mr Rawe then designed the St Piran dress tartan (vide) and to avoid confusion, Ms Abi Armstrong Evans changed the name of her tartan to Cornish Flag.

The Cornish Flag tartan was accredited by the Scottish Tartans Society in 1984, after a search of the Register of All Publicly Known Tartans had indicated that it was unique both in its setting and colour scheme. It has also been registered with the Design Registry (No. 514260) and cannot be reproduced without the designer's permission until protection lapses after due passage of time.

| **R** | bK | W | bK | **W** |
|---|---|---|---|---|
| 4 | 2 | 20 | 40 | 10 |

# CORNWALL
# (CORNISH HUNTING)

*Designer* Sandra A. Redwood

*Date* 1983

The Cornish hunting tartan was first produced in 1984 and was marketed by the firm of Cornovi Creations. It had been conceived by the firm's previous owner, Mrs Sandra Redwood. After consultation with the Scottish Tartans Society, she finalised the design with the help of Julia Redwood, William Charnock and Mr & Mrs John Charnock. The Cornish hunting tartan was designed for people who wish to wear a tartan which symbolises their loyalty to Cornwall, but which is more subdued than the Cornish national tartan. It incorporates all the colours associated with the latter, with the substitution of a dark green background in place of the gold, which is reduced to a narrow stripe. The azure blue of the national Cornish tartan is replaced with a dark blue.

The first 'pieces' of Cornish hunting tartan were produced by Lochcarron Mills of Galashiels in Scotland. Mr Michael Howarth, representing the mill, attended the public launch of the tartan on 20 March 1984. This was widely publicised in the local press and on local radio.

The Cornish hunting tartan has proved to be a popular tartan and is sometimes used for full length wedding dresses, rather than the more usual white. It has been registered with the Design Registry (No. 514267). It cannot be reproduced without the permission of the designer during the currency of the registration.

| R | bK | B | G | Y | bK | W |
|---|----|---|---|---|----|---|
| 6 | 6 | 14 | 48 | 4 | 52 | 10 |

# CORNWALL
# (ST PIRAN DRESS)

*Designer* Donald Rawe

*Date* 1984

The St Piran dress tartan is so called because it has a greater predominance of white than the St Piran. There is, however, no correlation between the two with regard to the setts but there is a personal connection which is of interest. The designer of the St Piran dress tartan, Mr Donald Rawe, was formerly associated with the design of the original St Piran tartan, subsequently to be known as the Cornish Flag tartan (see p. 140). However, he and Ms Abi Armstrong Evans subsequently decided to go their separate ways. Competition between the different tartan designers and weavers has played an important role in the development of tartans, and the two St Piran tartans are a good example of what can sometimes take place. Donald Rowe is also the designer of the Cornish National Day tartan.

The colours of the St Piran Dress tartan, black and white, have a dual significance. In a religious context, they are said to represent the white Light of Christ shining out from a dark world. In Cornish folklore, they indicate bright tin in contrast to dark mineral ore. St Piran is credited with having discovered the means by which tin can be smelted and he is the patron saint of tin miners. As with the St Piran tartan, the red represents the Cornish Chough, whilst the introduction of green denotes St Piran's Irish origin.

The St Piran dress tartan has been registered with the Design Registry (No. 514290) and cannot be reproduced without the permission of the designer during the currency of the registration.

| R | W | DG | W | DG | W | bK | **W** |
|---|---|---|---|---|---|----|---|
| 8 | 38 | 4 | 16 | 4 | 16 | 76 | 8 |

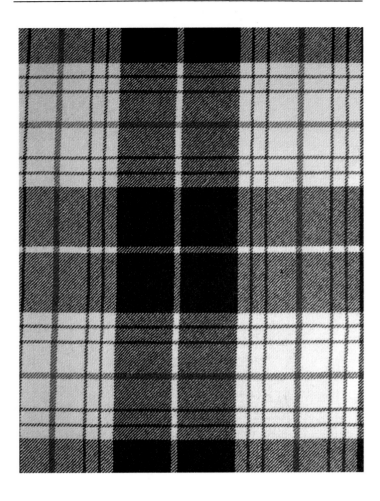

# DEVON

*Designer* Roy Sheard

*Date* 1984

Devon, as one of the counties of the South West Peninsula, is bounded by the sea to the north and south, by Somerset and Dorset to the east and by Cornwall to the west.

The Devon tartan owes its origin to the success of the Cornish St Piran sett, which was woven during the early 1980s at Coldharbour Mill in Devon. A number of Devonians, attracted by the symbolism of this Cornish tartan, asked Coldharbour Mill whether Devon, too, had a tartan of its own. To satisfy this need, Roy Sheard, who at that time worked for Coldharbour Mill Trust, designed the Devon tartan. This was subsequently accredited by the Council of the Scottish Tartans Society. The Certificate of Accreditation was formally presented by Dr Gordon Teall of Teallach to the Mayor of Barnstaple at a special ceremony in that town organised by Mr S. C. Coles in 1991. It is now worn by the North Devon Pipes and Drums.

Miss M. J. Miles has expressed the significance of the colours in her poem 'The Devon Tartan':

> Dark Green depicts wild Exmoor's windswept heights,
> And upland flocks of sheep are shown in white.
> Light green: lush meadows edged by sparkling stream
> Where graze producers of our milk and cream.
>
> Majestic Dartmoor, bleak and boulder-strewn,
> Its grim grandeur by grey on our cloth shown:
> There, ancient monuments gaze up to older tors,
> There, granite bound, the prison bars its doors.
>
> Ruby red cattle, deer and red soil, too,
> These are all there in stripe of red-brown hue.
> The yellow thread speaks of the primrose fair
> In high-banked lanes, midst wealth of plant life there.
>> So, in the mind, Devon's beauty is retrieved
>> By contemplating Devon's tartan's weave.

The Devon tartan is complementary to the Devon Companion.

| **LN** | MG | W | MG | T | DG | **Y** |
|--------|----|----|----|----|----|-------|
| 20 | 16 | 4 | 16 | 16 | 16 | 4 |

# DEVON COMPANION

*Designer* Roy Sheard

*Date* 1984

The success of the Devon tartan stimulated a demand for a further county tartan, in which the background was predominantly blue. Roy Sheard in consequence decided to create the Devon Companion. It was an apt choice of name; whereas the Devon, sometimes known as the Devon Original, had represented inland Devon, the Companion, by introducing a colour change, sought to emphasise the seafaring heritage of the coasts. The main background colours are two shades of blue, the lighter for the sea, the darker for the connection of Plymouth and Devonport with the Royal and Merchant Navies. The sands of Saunton and Woolacombe are denoted by the yellow, the cliffs at Sidmouth by the reddish brown, and the chalk cliffs by the white. The pronounced light grey serves to emphasise both the beautiful coastline around Hartland Point with its long promontories of rock which sweep down to the sea, and the well-known pebble ridge, two miles in length, at Westward Ho.

In order to stress the difference between Devon and Cornwall, the Devon Original and Devon Companion were at first woven in herringbone 2/2 broken twill which gave them a distinct appearance of their own sometimes described as the 'Devon weave'. This custom, however, is no longer always observed and the tartans are sometimes woven in the usual 2/2 plain twill in order to make them more suitable for the manufacture of kilts.

Roy Sheard has now retired from Cold Harbour Mill, but the Devon tartans are still woven at the mill by Colin Bates.

| LN | B | Y | B | bK | T | W |
|----|----|----|----|----|----|----|
| 20 | 16 | 4 | 16 | 16 | 16 | 4 |

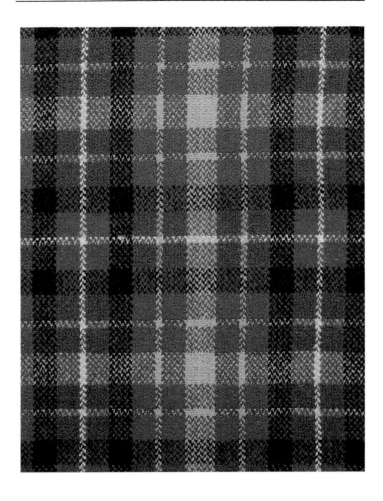

# DURHAM

*Designer* Wilsons of Bannockburn

*Date* 1819

Durham is the name of both the ancient English city of Durham and the county in which it is situated. Some thirty-two miles from the Scottish border, at its nearest point, the county suffered from many incursions by the Scots. The ancient earthworks, known as Scots dyke, run through Durham county for a quarter of its length. There is, however, no real historic reason why this English county should have a tartan of its own. Nevertheless, its entitlement to such a tartan has the same pedigree as many of the Scottish district tartans and indeed many clan tartans.

The Durham district tartan first appears in 1819 in the records of Wilsons of Bannockburn. It was the practice of this firm to give the names of towns or districts to many of their tartans. Exactly why the Durham sett was so called may always be a mystery. Maybe it sold well in Durham, or perhaps it was named after a purchaser of that surname.

The Durham district tartan has, however, become firmly established not entirely without reason. Much of the County of Durham is akin to that of Scotland, wild desolate moors, peat bogs and high hills. For walking in such an area the kilt is an ideal garment and for this reason alone the Durham tartan has its adherents.

| bK | G | bK | B | R | |
|----|----|----|----|----|-----|
| 4 | 12 | 12 | 12 | 4 | (1) |
| 6 | 16 | 18 | 19 | 6 | (2) |

# SOMERSET

*Designer* R. Sheard

*Date* 1984

The County of Somerset forms part of the southwestern peninsula of England, together with Devon and Cornwall. It has a
northern shore line along the Bristol Channel and is bounded by
Devon to the south and west. It is a district in which Celtic
memories linger on, a land of a legend where King Arthur, the
British king, battled against the Anglo-Saxon invaders in the
sixth century.

The Somerset district tartan is symbolic of the scenery of the
county. The blue represents the wide inland expanses of water
at Chatworthy, the rivers of mid-Somerset, the Parrett and the
Brue, and the sea into which they flow. The sandy-brown
represents the withies, or willows, which grow along the banks
of the drainage ditches known as Rhines, on the 'Plain of
Sedgemoor' and which are used for basket-making. The black
is a reminder of the peat which is to be found at Sedgemoor.
The grey is intended to portray the colour of much of the
building stone used in the area, in particular Glastonbury
Abbey, Wells Cathedral, and the three-sided monument to the
Duke of Wellington standing on the Blackdown hills overlooking the town of Wellington. The pink represents the
fragrant wild flowers known as the Cheddar Pink which grows
in the Cheddar Gorge. The flower was a favourite souvenir of
Victorian tourists which accounts for its rarity today. The
green portrays the green of the Quantock Hills and the wilderness of Exmoor.

Somerset may be regarded as the most English of all counties
for which a district tartan has been created by one of the local
residents. It remains to be seen whether the concept of modern
symbolic district tartan will spread elsewhere in England.

| G | N | A | Pk | T | bK | T | bK | **T** |
|---|---|---|----|---|----|---|----|---|
| 16 | 16 | 14 | 10 | 4 | 4 | 4 | 4 | 4 |

# TYNESIDE

*Designer* Unknown

*Date* 1914

Tyneside is an area steeped in the conflicts of yesteryear. The River Tyne and its tributaries drain much of northern England. The South Tyne flows northward from the Pennine Hills. The North Tyne rises in the Cheviot Hills on the Scottish border to pass through the line of Hadrian's Wall. This Roman fortification, still extant in many places, was commenced after Hadrian's visit in AD 122 and stretched from the Solway Firth in the west to the estuary of the Tyne in the east, being finally abandoned in 383. After the Romans had departed, the Tyneside area was to form part of the ancient kingdom of Northumbria which encompassed, as its zenith, what is now southeast Scotland and northeast England, from the Forth to the Humber.

Newcastle-upon-Tyne, a modern manufacturing and university city, is an important crossing place on the Tyne, being the site of the Roman settlement of Pons Aelii. Here too, the conquering Normans built the stronghold from which Newcastle derived its name. From the city to the sea, lies the industrial urban complex of Gateshead, ie Gateshead, Wallsend (the eastern end of Hadrian's Wall), Jarrow and Tyne-mouth.

The Tyneside tartan is not a district tartan in the sense that it was locally woven. At the beginning of the First World War in 1914, Lord Kitchener authorised the raising of a battalion, to be known as the Tyneside Scottish. The War Office would not agree to the wearing of tartan or the kilt by the rank and file, but permission to do so was given to the pipers of the 20th, 21st, 22nd and 23rd Battalions Northumberland Fusiliers. The pattern is a colour change based on the Black Watch (42nd) or Government sett, with tan replacing the usual black. In recent years, the sett has come to be regarded as a suitable district tartan for those connected with Tyneside. Such a change of use is not unique since much the same happened in the case of the Sutherland district tartan.

| **B** | T | B | T | B | T | G | T | G | T | B | T | **B** |
|-------|---|---|---|---|---|---|---|---|---|---|---|-------|
| 40 | 6 | 6 | 6 | 6 | 34 | 34 | 6 | 34 | 34 | 34 | 6 | 6 |

# MANX NATIONAL
# (ELLAN VANNIN)

*Designers* Patricia McQuaid and D. Gordon Teall of Teallach

*Date* 1958

The Isle of Man, in the centre of the Irish Sea, is a land of great beauty. It is a dependency of the British Crown and has its own parliament, Tynwald. The island was settled by Gaels in about AD 450 and a strong Celtic tradition persists upon this proudly independent island to the present day. Tartan, in the form of simple checks, was probably traditionally woven upon the island for centuries. More complicated designs were produced in St Judes and Andreas in the nineteenth century, mainly in connection with blankets and quilts, but no specific names seem to have been given to them.

The idea of a Manx national tartan was first put forward by Lord Sempill in 1957 at a meeting of Ellynyn ny Gael (the Art of the Gaels). The design eventually chosen was that of Miss Patricia McQuaid, a well-known handweaver on the island. She took the colours of the island's scenery as her theme subsequently to be expressed in a poem by Ewan Kelly:

> Ligh blue for the sea in the shimmering sunlight
> Green for the hills which slope down to the sea.
> Purple for heather on far distant mountain.
> Gold for the gorse so richly endowed.
> Brown for the bracken in quiet lane and bye-way.
> White for cottages so snug and content,
> Dark blue the shadows that play on the waters.
> All these are the colours which nature has shown
> To make up the tartan of our island home.

The Manx National tartan was subsequently redesigned by Dr Gordon Teall of Teallach to make it more suitable for modern weaving techniques. This tartan has been accredited by the Scottish Tartans Society and is a Registered Trade Design.

| **P** | G | R | Y | B | A | **W** |
|----|----|---|---|----|----|---|
| 8 | 31 | 4 | 4 | 17 | 64 | 4 |

# ISLE OF MAN

*Designer* T. Richard Moore

*Date* 1975

The Isle of Man tartan owes its origin to a disagreement with regard to the commercial weaving of the Manx national tartan, the first samples of which had been produced by its designer, Miss Patricia McQuaid, on a hand-loom. She had registered her Manx national design in 1959 under the Registered Designs Act, and reached an agreement with the Tynwald Woollen Mills at St John's to produce it commercially in the form of rugs. Differing views, concerning the supervision of production, however, led to an eventual termination of the arrangement. The Mills nevertheless continued to receive enquiries about the Manx national tartan. In consequence, in 1975 it was decided to produce an entirely new tartan which could be identified with the Isle of Man. Thus, was born the Isle of Man tartan, designed by Mr T. Richard Moore, who had been associated with the Tynwald mills for more than fifty years. He, like Miss McQuaid, based his tartan on the colours prevalent on the island, expressing his ideas in the form of a poem:

> The Misty-Blue for the seas that surround
> The Reddy-Brown for the rocks that abound
> The Green for the grass and Green for the trees
> The Gold for the gorse that waves in the breeze
> The White for the cottages, homely and gay
> The Red for the sunset at close of the day
> The Purple, the heather that covers the hills
> THE ISLE OF MAN TARTAN from Tynwald Mills.

| **R** | A | T | W | G | Y | G | W | G | P | Y | P | **W** |
|---|---|---|---|---|---|---|---|---|---|---|---|---|
| 2 | 22 | 4 | 3 | 7 | 2 | 4 | 2 | 9 | 6 | 2 | 4 | 2 |

# ISLE OF MAN (LAXEY MANX)

*Designer* Robert Wood

*Date* 1978

The Laxey Manx is another tartan which owes its origin to differences of opinion between Miss Patricia McQuaid, the designer of the Manx national tartan, and a commercial producer. Whereas the Tynwald Woollen Mills had been concerned with Miss McQuaid's design in the form of rugs, it was the St George's Woollen Mills at Laxey to which she had given orders for its production as a tweed suitable for the manufacture of clothing. After initial production runs, acrimony developed, however, between the parties concerned, which eventually led to the weaving of the Manx national tartan being undertaken by another company off the island.

The growing popularity of the Manx national and Isle of Man tartans, particularly amongst visitors to the island, however, was destined to become a challenge to Mr Robert Wood, the proprietor of the St George's Woollen Mills. An experienced weaver, he decided to produce his own tartan in 1978, calling it the Laxey Manx to prevent confusion with its two rivals. In general appearance, his design bore a greater resemblance to Miss McQuaid's original than did the Isle of Man tartan. It comprised only six colours, the red being omitted. This simplified the weaving and produced an aesthetically pleasing tartan which has become to be regarded as one of the 'national' tartans of the Isle of Man.

| **B** | G | Y | P | B | **W** |
|-------|-----|-----|-----|-----|-------|
| 8 | 32 | 4 | 14 | 56 | 8 |

# SNAEFELL

*Designer* Robert Wood

*Date* 1979

Snaefell (the Snow Mountain) is the highest mountain on the Isle of Man. Rising over two thousand feet in height it has a commanding position above the Irish Sea. For this reason, radio communication masts have been built near its summit, adding to its height and making it easy to identify from a distance. On a clear day six kingdoms can be seen from its peak, England, Ireland, Man, Scotland, Wales and, as local residents will add with a smile, the Kingdom of Heaven.

The summit can be reached either on foot or by the mountain railway which climbs to a small mountain top non-residential hotel. The electric train or tram, as some prefer to call it, winds its way up the glen from the old mining village of Laxey. In summer the railway attracts many thousands of passengers. As one drives down the hill into Laxey from Ramsey, Snaefell can clearly be seen dominating the skyline above the village. It is not surprising, therefore, that the mountain was to give its name to a district tartan manufactured by St George's Woollen Mills at its foot. Introduced in 1979, the Snaefell tartan represents the bracken of the mountainside, covered with winter snow. It is based on part of the Black Watch tartan, and is precisely the same sett as is recorded for the family Turnbury, in the Register of All Known Tartans of the Scottish Tartans Society. It has proved to be a very popular tartan, particularly for women's costumes and skirts.

| **LT** | DT | LT | DT | LT | DT | W | **DT** |
|--------|----|----|----|----|----|----|----|
| 44 | 4 | 4 | 4 | 4 | 30 | 34 | 6 |

# MANX HUNTING

*Designers* C. Ewan Kelly and D. Gordon Teall of Teallach

*Date* 1980

The Manx hunting tartan owes its origin to the demand for a design which was not so bright as the original Manx national tartan and therefore more suitable for people, particularly men, who might prefer subdued colours. The need for a separate hunting tartan on these grounds is not necessarily justified because tartans which are vivid when woven in modern colours, or even ancient, become 'quiet' when woven in reproduction or muted colours. In this case, however, there was also the desire for an alternative design — the 'Webb of Manannan':

> Dark grey — the rocks; the heart of Ellan Vannin;
> Grey green — her rugged valleys, hills and moors;
> Clear blue — the sky above the land of Mannin,
> Grey blue — the sea around her shining shores,
> Bright gold — the gleam of cushag flowers a-blowing;
> Pure white — the mist that lingers for a whole;
> These, woven on the Loom of Love are showing
> The soft lived fabric of Manannan's Isle.

The Manx hunting tartan was produced after agreement between Mr C. Ewan Kelly, who marketed the Manx national tartan, and D. Gordon Teall of Teallach, joint author of this book. Mr Kelly, had a preliminary sketch for such a tartan, which was developed by Dr Teall in consultation with Loch Carron Weavers of Galashiels.

This tartan has been accredited by the Scottish Tartans Society and is a Registered Trade Design.

| **A** | DG | G | DG | Y | DG | W | DG | N | DG | **B** |
|-------|----|----|----|----|----|----|----|----|----|-------|
| 12 | 2 | 40 | 2 | 8 | 2 | 8 | 2 | 22 | 2 | 76 |

# LAXEY (CENTENARY)

*Designer* Robert Wood

*Date* 1981

The Laxey (Centenary) tartan may be regarded as the district tartan for Laxey village, with special emphasis upon the part played in the history of the local community by the St George's Woollen Mills. Laxey is a beautiful village situated on the east coast of the Isle of Man. Its small harbour, situated at the mouth of the Laxey River, is a haven for local yachtmen. When the tide recedes, and the harbour dries out, around the harbour mole an extensive sandy beach appears beyond the pebbles of the foreshore, which in summer is thronged with holiday-makers. This is a village where lead mining was the principal industry in the nineteenth century, during which period the famous Isabella wheel, one of the largest waterwheels in the world, was built to pump water from the mines. It is now a tourist attraction.

In 1881, John Rudkin, the famous philanthropist, founded the St George's Woollen Mills to relieve hardship in the village. One of the main products of the mills in their early days was grey flannel which was extensively worn at that time. In order to commemorate the centenary of the founding of the mills in 1981, the Laxey Centenary tartan was introduced. This has a grey background to represent the grey flannel upon which is superimposed the blue and green of the Manx (Laxey) tartan. it is a popular tartan, both with local residents and tourists.

| **B** | G | B | G | B | G | N | G | **N** |
|-------|---|---|---|---|---|----|---|----|
| 44 | 6 | 6 | 6 | 6 | 18 | 56 | 6 | 12 |

# CLODAGH

*Designer* Unknown

*Date* c.1970

Clodagh is the name of both hamlet and river in the West Riding of Cork in southwest Ireland. The hamlet is situated in the parish of Drimoleague (Drom-da-Liag). The Clodagh river rises near Nowen Hill and its valley is a district of peaceful beauty. It joins the River Ilen which flows down to the sea near Skibbereen.

How this particular tartan became to be regarded as the Clodagh district tartan will probably always remain in doubt. The earliest sample known to the Scottish Tartans Society was woven by D. C. Dalgleish of Selkirk in 1970 or thereabouts. In 1979, a bagpipe maker, Andrew S. Warnock from Co. Tyrone in Northern Ireland, wrote to Alex Lumsden, a Research Fellow of the Scottish Tartans Society, stating that he knew the tartan as Clodnaugh Irish and that it had 'been established that it originated somewhere in the Bog of Allen in Southern Ireland'. The bog, however, is situated to the West of Dublin and is some 150 miles from Clodagh. The story may be mythical and it is possible that the tartan is a relatively modern fashion design. The mystery already surrounding the original of Clodagh district tartan, however, is an interesting example of the romance that sometimes attaches itself to tartan.

The sett is based upon that of the Royal Stewart and is very similar to other named variations of that widely known tartan, particularly the King George VI and Macbeth. Whatever its origins, the tartan has become popular, especially in the United States, with people having connections with the South of Ireland.

| W | B | Y | bK | W | bK | W | bK | G | T | bK | T | W |
|---|---|---|----|---|----|---|----|---|---|----|---|---|
| 6 | 40 | 8 | 18 | 6 | 6 | 6 | 6 | 28 | 18 | 6 | 8 | 6 |

# TARA

*Designer* Unknown

*Date* c.1880

The Hill of Tara lies to the west of the main road from Dublin (Baile Atha Cliath) to Navan (An Uaimh). Over five hundred feet in height the hill occupies a commanding position in the central Irish plain. It is an emotive place which conjures up visions of Ireland's historic past. Its importance probably goes back to the Bronze Age and it was certainly a sacred site for the early Celts. It is referred to as 'the supreme seat of the monarch of Ireland' in the tenth-century Book of Rights. It achieved this position because in the early Christian era the five kingdoms of Ireland had formed themselves into two groups, the northern one led by the king of Tara, the southern by the king of Munster. As a spirit of national consciousness steadily developed, the king of Tara had become recognised as the high king (ard-ri).

It has not been possible to establish a local connection in Ireland for the Tara district tartan. Its thread count, however, was noted in *Clans Originaux* by T. Claude Fresklie which was published in Paris in c.1880. The tartan was then known by the family name of Murphy. The date of the appending of the name Tara is uncertain but it was ordered as such from the Kilt Shop in Edinburgh by an Irish customer in 1967.

The Tara tartan is virtually a colour change on the MacLean of Duart tartan, which in turn is a variation of the Royal Stewart. It is a popular tartan today, for people of Irish ancestry who have connections within the area around Tara and also for people from Meath and the other counties which comprise the province of Leinster.

| **bK** | G | R | G | T | bK | W | bK | Y | bK | R | **bK** |
|----|---|---|----|----|----|---|----|---|----|---|----|
| 4 | 6 | 4 | 52 | 20 | 4 | 6 | 4 | 4 | 6 | 4 | 16 |

# ULSTER

*Designer* Not known

*Date* Late sixteenth or early seventeenth century

Ulster was one of the five states of early Celtic Ireland. During Norman times, it was an earldom comprising approximately the area included in the present counties of Antrim and Down. At the present time, confusion is caused because the word 'Ulster' is often used to refer to the political entity of Northern Ireland, which forms part of the United Kingdom and comprises the Counties of Down, Antrim, Armagh, Fermanagh, Londonderry and Tyrone. Historically, however, Ulster also includes the three counties of the Republic of Ireland, Cavan, Monaghan and Donegal.

The Ulster tartan, as it is known today, owes its origin to the discovery on the 23 April 1956, of remnants of clothing buried beside a lane leading to a farm known as 'The Hill', Flanders Townland, about a mile north of Dungiven in County Londonderry. The farmer, Mr W. G. Dixon, took the clothing to the Belfast Museum and Art Gallery. Examination showed that the garments, dating from between 1590 and 1650, comprised a semi-circular woollen cloak, a tunic, trews, belt and shoes. The trews were made from a fine and regular 2/2, Z spun, tartan twill with occasional reversals to the pattern to form a herringbone. The colours had stained to various shades of brown, but where best preserved, seemed to have comprised four colours, red, dull green, darker brown and orange or yellow. The ground consisted of wide blocks of red and green, divided by narrow lines of orange, dark brown and green. The repeat of the warp stripes was not absolutely regular but the weft was more constant.

The clothing seems to have lain in a shallow ditch or sheugh which filled with dark peaty loam with a sub-soil of turf. This had the effect of staining the garment a deep reddish brown. The modern Ulster tartan is based on the general appearance of the stained fabric and has an overall tan appearance.

| bK | R | bK | DT | bK | LT | bK | LT | bK | LT |
|----|----|----|----|----|----|----|----|----|----|
| 4 | 4 | 4 | 58 | 4 | 4 | 4 | 56 | 4 | 56 |

# WELSH NATIONAL

*Designer* D. M. Richards

*Date* 1967

Wales, a nation of the United Kingdom, has a long and often violent history which became less turbulent after it became fully united with England in the sixteenth century. The Principality of Wales is renowned for its mountains, Offa's Dyke and medieval castles. Its world-famous coalmines, the product of the Industrial Revolution, are today declining in numbers to be replaced in the Welsh economy by modern technological industries.

A land of song, poetry and drama, its national eisteddfods are highly regarded. Spoken Welsh language is soft and lilting and great efforts are made today to keep it a living language at a time when English is becoming the medium of international communication.

The word 'Welsh' derives from the Anglo-Saxon *wælisc*, meaning foreign. It was as foreigners that the Anglo-Saxon invaders regarded the Welsh speaking Celtic people of western Britain.

The feeling of separate nationhood speaks today and the Welsh tartan is symbolic in this respect. The Welsh tartan owes its origin to a Society formed in Cardiff in 1967. Its aims were mainly cultural, but partly political:

1. To be fully united with other Celtic countries
2. To preserve the particular identity of the Welsh nation
3. To strengthen Celtic ties and to give visible signs of being an individual nation in culture, language and dress
4. To make every endeavour to allow Wales to have greater and more individual representation in the affairs of the United Kingdom.

In pursuance of these aims, this Welsh Society designed a tartan for a national Welsh kilt. The colours selected were those of the Welsh flag, a red dragon on a green and white background.

| C | LG | C | LG | W |
|----|----|----|----|----|
| 16 | 8 | 8 | 80 | 8 |

# SECTION IV
# OTHER DISTRICT TARTANS

## CONTENTS

**AUSTRALIA**
Australia 178

**BAHAMAS**
Bahamas 180

**BERMUDA**
Bermuda 182

**CANADA**
Alberta 184
British Columbia 186
Bruce County 188
Canadian Centennial 190
Canada (Maple Leaf) 192
Cape Breton 194
Essex County 196
Fredericton 198
Manitoba 200
New Brunswick 202
Newfoundland 204
North West Territories 206
Nova Scotia 208
Ontario (Ensign of) 210

**CANADA** *contd.*
Ottawa 212
Prince Edward Island 214
Quebec 216
Saskatchewan 218
Yukon 220

**UNITED STATES OF AMERICA**
American Tartan 222
America (St Andrews) 224
Carolina 226
Dunedin 228
Georgia 230
Idaho (Centennial) 232
Maine 234
Ohio 236
Texas (Bluebonnet) 238
Tulsa 240
Washington 242

**NETHERLANDS**
Dutch 244

# AUSTRALIA

*Designer* John Reid

*Date* 1984

Australia has a long but obscure pre-history. Evidence suggests three principal migratory incursions by primitive man, but the modern history of the continent does not begin until the advent of the Europeans. There is some evidence that the French, or more probably the Portuguese, raided the western coasts during the sixteenth century. The first authenticated records do not begin till almost a century later, when it was visited by the Dutch. The eastern coast remained unknown until 1770 when Captain Cook entered what is now Botany Bay to proclaim the colony of New South Wales.

The War of American Independence hastened the colonisation of Australia. It forced the British Government to look for new lands to which to transport convicts. The early years of the settlement, which included free men, brought much strife and rivalry between the officers appointed to rule the colony. Eventually, in 1809, Lachlan MacQuarie, who was born on the island of Ulva, Argyll, took up office as Governor. He retired in 1821 having brought regular civil government to the colony, earning for himself the accolade of 'Father of Australia'.

Not all Australians, even those of Scots descent, can claim a tartan associated with their family name. Consequently, in 1984, the Scottish Australian Heritage Council decided to hold a competition for the design of an Australia Pattern. The winner was John Reid, an architect from Melbourne. The winning pattern makes use of the five colours of the land, most used by the Australian Aborigines — ochre, red/brown, black, white and cobalt blue. This gives the tartan an overall 'warm' appearance, reminiscent of the great outback. The tartan is formed by a colour change of the MacQuarie sett with two additional lines; an alternate white/blue line in the centre of the broad band and a black line between the thin band. It is a Registered Design in Australia (No. 97439).

| **B** | T | LT | T | LT | bK | LT | T | LT | T | LT | bK | LT | T | LT | T | **W** |
|---|---|---|---|---|---|---|---|---|---|---|---|---|---|---|---|---|
| 4 | 30 | 20 | 8 | 5 | 4 | 4 | 8 | 100 | 8 | 4 | 4 | 4 | 8 | 20 | 30 | 4 |

# BAHAMAS

*Designer* Gordon Rees
*Date* 1966

The Bahamas is an independent state within the Commonwealth of which the Queen is the Head. They comprise a chain of approximately seven hundred islands, some 600 miles in length, terminating within 72 miles of the coast of Florida. Only twenty-one of the islands are inhabited. The Bahamas were discovered by Christopher Columbus in 1492 and had a chequered history during the seventeenth and eighteenth centuries being governed alternately by the British and Spanish. The islands became British in 1783.

The Bahamas tartan was designed in 1966 by the late Mr Gordon Rees of the Scottish Shop at Nassau, now owned by Colin and Beverley Honnes. It was intended to perpetuate the memory of the early Scottish settlers in the Bahamas and to represent the natural beauty of the country. Each colour has a meaning as shown below:

| *Colour* | *In memory of the name* | *Associated Scottish Clan* |
|---|---|---|
| Blue for the | Thompson | MacThomas & Campbell |
| Sea and Sky | Sands | Fifeshire family |
| Green for the | Forsythe | Lamont |
| Foliage | Munroe | Munroe |
| | Johnston | Gunn and MacIan |
| | Johnstone | Johnston |
| | Russell | Cumming |
| Red for the | Christie | Farquharson |
| sun | Roberts | Robertson |
| | Kelly | MacDonald |
| | MacKinney | MacKenzie |
| | Saunders | MacAlister |
| Yellow for the | Malcolm | Malcolm and MacCallum |
| Beaches and the | Crawford | Lindsay |
| White for the | MacPherson | MacPherson |
| clouds and the | Clark | MacKintosh |
| Moon | Rae | MacRae |

The Bahamas tartan was given formal approval by the Bahamas Government in August 1966.

| B | G | W | R | G | B | Y | B |
|---|---|---|---|---|---|---|---|
| 6 | 22 | 22 | 4 | 14 | 44 | 4 | 4 |

# BERMUDA

*Designer* Peter Macarthur

*Date* 1962

Bermuda lies in the West Atlantic Ocean and is regarded as Britain's oldest colony. It is a Dependent Territory and comprises some 150 small islands, of which only approximately twenty are inhabited. The chain of islands are some 22 miles long and are situated about 580 miles east of North Carolina in the USA. Many of the Islands, which are of coral formation, are linked by bridges and causeways. Bermuda is named after the Spaniard Juan de Bermudez, who visited the islands in 1515. British settlers, however, established a colony there in 1609. Bermuda has an expanding tourist industry and its capital Hamilton is developing as an important finance cnetre.

There are two Bermudan District tartans:

The original Bermuda Plaid was designed by Peter Macarthur Limited of Hamilton, Scotland in 1962 and was marketed on the island by Trimmingham Bros. Ltd.

Shortly afterwards a second Bermudan tartan, known as Bermuda Blue was developed by Peter Hamilton from the design of Mr N. H. P. Vesey, Jr. the President of H. A. & E. Smith of Bermuda. This tartan is symbolic and represents:

| | |
|---|---|
| Dark Blue | Water |
| Lt. Blue | Sky |
| Red | Coral |
| Green | Cedar trees endemic to the islands |

*Bermuda (Plaid)*

| A | B | A | G | B | R | A |
|---|---|---|---|---|---|---|
| 16 | 4 | 16 | 24 | 24 | 16 | 66 |

*Bermuda (Blue)*

| LB | R | DB | LB | R | LB | DB | LB | DG | LB | R | LB | DB |
|----|---|----|----|---|----|----|----|----|----|---|----|----|
| 12 | 4 | 4 | 42 | 6 | 6 | 11 | 6 | 19 | 8 | 4 | 6 | 6 |

# ALBERTA

*Designers* Mrs A. Lamb and Mrs E. Neilsen

*Date* 1961

Alberta is an inland prairie province with arbitrary boundaries drawn along lines of longitude and latitude, with the exception of part of the western border which follows the watershed of the Rocky Mountains in a southeasterly direction as far as the United States frontier. Its capital is Edmonton.

The Alberta tartan is intended to symbolise the natural assets of the province:

> Green for our forest,
> Gold for our wheat and sunshine,
> Blue for our lakes and the clear skies above,
> Black for our oil and coal,
> Pink for our floral emblem, the wild rose.

The predominant colours of the tartan, green and gold are those adopted by the province.

The Alberta tartan was developed by the Edmonton Rehabilitation Society, a voluntary agency, in order to provide a worthwhile project for handicapped students learning to operate handlooms at the Society's Rehabilitation Centre. It was designed by two Alberta women, Mrs Alison Lamb, executive director of the Edmonton Rehabilitation Society and Mrs Ellen Neilsen, its weaving instructress. The tartan is still being woven at the Centre, now known as the Goodwill Rehabilitation Services of Alberta.

The Provincial Legislative of Alberta gave formal approval for the Alberta tartan in March 1961.

| G | bK | LR | bK | A | bK | Y |
|---|----|----|----|---|----|---|
| 24 | 2 | 2 | 2 | 4 | 2 | 8 |

# BRITISH COLUMBIA

*Designer* Eric K. Ward

*Date* 1966

British Columbia is bordered by the North West Territories and Yukon to the north, Alberta to the east, the United States to the south and the Pacific Ocean and the Alaska pan-handle to the west. The greater part of the population is British by descent. Apart from an area of lowland in the north-east, the province is a picturesque blend of mountain, plateau and valley. Large areas of land are forested and along the coast are magnificent fiords and islands, the largest of which is Vancouver Island. Much of the Province is reminiscent of the Highlands of Scotland, though drawn to a larger scale, being dominated by the Rocky Mountains to the east. Fishing, lumbering and mining are major industries to which may be added the secondary manufacturing businesses arising from them. Victoria is the capital and Vancouver the largest town.

The British Columbia Provincial tartan was produced by the Pik Mills of Quebec in connection with the Centennial Celebration of 1966 which marked the unification of the administration of the mainland and Vancouver Island a hundred years earlier.

| G | bK | G | A | Y | A | R | bK | R | A | R | W |
|---|----|---|---|---|---|---|----|---|---|---|---|
| 8 | 2 | 16 | 16 | 2 | 16 | 16 | 2 | 16 | 4 | 16 | 2 |

# BRUCE COUNTY

*Designer* Lord Bruce

*Date* 1964

Bruce County is an administrative district of the Province of Ontario. It takes its name from James Bruce, the Eighth Earl of Elgin and Kincardine, who was Governor General of Canada during a survey of the unsettled lands which subsequently formed the County of Bruce.

The County of Bruce attained its administrative status in 1867 and the development of its district tartan formed part of the Centennial celebrations in 1967. The suggestion of a tartan for the county was first made by one of its former wardens, Dr J. F. Morton of Southampton. This was taken up by the Bruce County Women's Institute on 18 October 1962 and a report was submitted to the county council in the following January. On 31 October 1963 the county council passed a byelaw establishing a tartan committee. A member of this committee, Mr Norman MacLeod, suggested approaching the Earl of Elgin and Kincardine, the Chief of the Clan Bruce seeking permission to adopt the sett of the Bruce tartan but with a variation of colour. Lord Bruce, Lord Elgin's son, acceded to the request on behalf of his father, stating that the Lord Lyon had suggested modifying the Bruce tartan by the inclusion of blue guard lines on either side of the white stripe. Blue had been suggested because the County has a long coastline of three hundred and sixty-seven miles stretching along Lake Huron and Georgian Bay.

The County Council subsequently approved the tartan and a formal presentation and dedication ceremony took place at Southampton on 10 July 1965.

| **W** | B | R | G | R | G | R | G | R | G | R | **Y** |
|-------|---|----|---|---|----|---|----|---|---|----|-------|
| 2 | 2 | 14 | 4 | 4 | 12 | 2 | 12 | 4 | 4 | 16 | 2 |

# CANADIAN CENTENNIAL

*Designers* 'Centennial Tartan'

*Date* 1966

The development of district tartans in Canada has been primarily motivated by loyalty to a specific province, since in general people wish to identify with the area in which they live, or where they or their forefathers were born. Thus, few Canadian tartans were designed with the whole of the Dominion in mind. One such exception is the Canadian Centennial. This was originated from Vancouver with a view to commemorating the 100th anniversary of the creation of the Dominion of Canada, under the British North America Act of 1867, by the British Government in Westminster. It was the only tartan of that name to receive the formal approval of the Centennial Commission.

Canadian Centennial tartan is woven in six colours chosen for their symbolism. The blue and green background and the narrow black and yellow lines portray the natural resources of Canada. The red and white stripes represent the Canadian flag. It could be argued that the Centennial tartan is a commemorative rather than a district tartan but the distinction is fine. It is now a district tartan representing the whole of Canada, but with particular emphasis on the political unity of the country.

| **R** | W | R | G | B | bK | B | **Y** |
|-------|-----|-----|-----|-----|-----|-----|-----|
| 6 | 12 | 4 | 64 | 72 | 4 | 8 | 4 |

# CANADA (MAPLE LEAF)

*Designer* David Weiser

*Date* 1964

The Canadian Maple Leaf tartan was created in anticipation of the centennary of the granting of Dominion status to Canada in 1867. The name Maple Leaf was chosen as maples are indigenous to Canada and the leaf, a symbol of nationhood, forms the central feature of the new Canadian flag, introduced in 1965. It was designed as a commercial venture by a Canadian, who had been in the fashion world for many years.

In the words of the Commercial Division of the Office of the High Commissioner for Canada —

> 'In creating the Maple Leaf Tartan fabric, David Weiser captured the natural phenomena of these leaves turning from summer into autumn. The green is the early colour of the foliage. Gold appears at the turn of autumn. Red shows up for the coming of the first frost. The two tones of brown find their way throughout the leaf creating a prolific profusion of colour.'

It may now be regarded as a national tartan.

| DG | R | DG | R | MG | R | DG | R | DG | T | MG | Y . . . |
|----|---|----|---|----|---|----|---|----|---|----|---------|
| 48 | 8 | 8 | 32 | 32 | 32 | 8 | 8 | 48 | 16 | 16 | 16 |

# CAPE BRETON

*Designer* Mrs Elizabeth Grant

*Date* 1957

Cape Breton, the island to the North of Nova Scotia, is one of the most historic districts of Canada. When by the Treaty of Utrecht in 1713, Nova Scotia was ceded back to Great Britain, Cape Breton remained French. Subsequently in 1755, those of French origin, the Acadians, were driven out of Nova Scotia. Cape Breton was given a separate administration in 1784 but rejoined Nova Scotia in 1819.

Cape Breton is one of those areas that is emotive and in 1907 Mrs Lillian Crewe Walsh of Glace Bay expressed her feeling about it in a poem:

> Black for the wealth of our coal mines,
>   Grey for our Cape Breton steel,
> Green for our lofty mountains,
>   Our valleys and our fields;
> Gold for the golden sunsets
>   Shining bright on the lakes of Bras d'Or
> To show us God's hand has lingered
>   To bless Cape Breton shores.

Some fifty years later, in 1957, the poem inspired her friend, Mrs Elizabeth Grant, also of Glace Bay, to design a tartan to accord with the colours of the poem. It has now become accepted by the local populace as their district tartan. The four colours are also symbolic of the four counties of Cape Breton, Richmond, Cape Breton county, Inverness and Victoria.

| **Y** | bK | G | bK | Grey | bK | **Y** |
|-------|----|----|----|------|----|-------|
| 10 | 10 | 34 | 12 | 48 | 12 | 6 |

# ESSEX COUNTY

*Designer* Mrs Edyth Baker

*Date* 1983

The County of Essex is an administrative division of the Province of Ontario. It is a rich agricultural area where many varieties of cereals are grown. Horticulture is likewise well established within the county which has been nicknamed 'The Tomato Capital of the World'. Saltmining, fishing and automotive manufacturing are also to be numbered amongst its industries.

The Essex County tartan was designed by Mrs Edyth C. Baker, who died in 1985 aged 83. She chose the colours to symbolise the beauty and wealth of this section of Canada:

| | |
|---|---|
| Golden Yellow | (Sunshine) for the various cereal crops. |
| Green | Spring fields, peas and produce. |
| Red | Tomatoes, fruits and flag. |
| Blue | Skies and waterways. |
| Black | Automotive industry. |
| White | Saltmines and fish. |

The Corporation of the County of Essex formally adopted the tartan on 4 April 1984 and it was also approved by the local Leamington Council. It was registered in Ottawa in 1984 and has been formally accredited by the Council of the Scottish Tartans Society.

| **W** | R | A | DG | MG | LG | bK | R | bK | **Y** |
|---|---|---|---|---|---|---|---|---|---|
| 4 | 4 | 12 | 8 | 10 | 6 | 2 | 8 | 2 | 60 |

# FREDERICTON

*Designers* The Loomcrofters

*Date* 1967

Fredericton is the capital city of New Brunswick and the administrative centre of York County. It takes its name from Prince Frederick, the second son of King George III. It is a cathedral city and is situated on the navigable St John river. The city crest includes both the Royal Ensign and the Union Jack. The loomcrofters of Fredericton, men and women who weave in their own homes on their own looms, were responsible for the creation of the tartan. They explain its significance thus:

*The Green Block*
Green for the forests from which Fredericton was carved and for the trees which line her streets. Gold for the Royal Prince and the Royal Ensign. Red, white and blue from the Union Jack.

The arrangement of the blue and white in the outer corners indicate the symmetry of the street plan in the heart of the city.

*The White Block*
Because this is a 'dress' tartan the background is white, which is centred by the Cathedral cross in the Bishop's colour purple. The cross is outlined in the blue of the river.

Unifying the two main blocks is the red for loyalty to Crown and Country and of New Brunswick University.

The colours of the seasons and the purple of the provincial flower, the violet, are here as well.

| **P** | A | W | R | G | A | W | A | W | A | G | **Y** |
|---|---|---|---|---|---|---|---|---|---|---|---|
| 6 | 2 | 18 | 12 | 10 | 4 | 4 | 4 | 4 | 4 | 24 | 4 |

# MANITOBA

*Designer* Hugh Kirkwood Rankine

*Date* 1962

Manitoba is one of Canada's prairie provinces, bordering upon Hudson Bay to the northeast. The history and natural resources of the area have been capsulated in the Manitoba tartan. The Department of Industry and Commerce explain the significance of the colours thus:

*Dark Red Squares* — for the Red River Settlement, now the City of Winnipeg, which was founded at the forks of the Red and Assiniboine Rivers in the Province of Manitoba in 1812, by Highland crofters.

*Azure Blue Lines* — for Thomas Douglas, Fifth Earl of Selkirk — incorporating a colour from the Douglas tartan — who recruited the crofters.

*Green Squares* — for the rich natural resources of the province — farm lands, forests, minerals, fisheries and water power.

*Golden Lines* — for the grain crops — Miles Macdonnel, leader of the first party of Selkirk Settlers planted some winter wheat by hand at the forks of the Red and Assiniboine rivers in the fall of 1812.

*Dark Green Lines* — for the men and women of many races who have enriched the life of the province.

The design of the tartan, after having been recorded in the Lyon Court Book by the Lord Lyon King of Arms, was approved by the Legislative Assembly of the Province of Manitoba under Bill No. 126 (Eliz) '62 and received Royal Assent on 1 May 1962. This tartan is sometimes depicted with the dark green as red. This is an example of the errors that can be caused by the Lord Lyon's use of heraldic colours to describe tartans. In heraldry G, gules, is red whereas G in the Scottish Tartan Society's Register of All Publicly Known Tartans is green.

The sett illustrated shows the dark green intended by the designer.

| A | LG | A | LG | DG | LG | Maroon | Y |
|---|----|---|----|----|----|--------|---|
| 4 | 2  | 2 | 24 | 4  | 2  | 12     | 4 |

# NEW BRUNSWICK

*Designer* The Loomcrofters

*Date* 1959

New Brunswick is one of the Maritime Provinces of Canada. Compact in shape, it has a long coastline. The natural vegetation is forest, although much of the land has been cleared for farming. The rough uplands, heavily wooded, provide attractive scenery which is popular with tourists.

The New Brunswick tartan was commissioned by Lord Beaverbrook and was formally adopted by the Province by an order of the Lieutenant-Governor-in-Council made on 30 April 1959. Subsequently this order was recorded in the Books of the Court of the Lord Lyon (writs section).

The significance of the colours of the tartan are as follows:

| | |
|---|---|
| Beaver Brown | to perpetuate the name of Lord Beaverbrook. |
| Red | to signify the loyalty and devotion to the Crown and Country of the Loyalist settlers, the New Brunswick regiments and the people of the province. |
| Grey & Gold | to represent the coat of arms of the province. |
| Blue | to symbolise the rivers of the province. |
| Field Green | to illustrate the shade of growing crops. |
| Forest Green | to make the contrast in colour of the forest canopy. |

The tartan as recorded by the Order of the Lieutenant-Governor-in-Council comprises four blocks with a total of 760 ends or threads before the sequence is repeated. The resulting asymmetric tartan is extraordinarily complicated with the result that commercial weavers have tended to produce a simplified version.

The full thread count as recorded in the Lyon Court Book, is given on p.246.

# NEWFOUNDLAND

*Designer* Louis Anderson

*Date* 1972

Newfoundland, an island with an area slightly less than that of England, occupies a strategic position at the entrance to the Gulf of St Lawrence. It has a long history, having been visited by John Cabot in 1497 during the reign of Henry VIII. More than half the island is afforested and there are large areas of barren plateau. In consequence, agriculture is not one of the island's major industries, which include fishing, mining and lumbering together with the secondary industries arising therefrom, in particular the manufacture of pulp and paper.

The colours of the Newfoundland tartan are related to the 'Ode to Newfoundland', the second anthem of the province:

| | |
|---|---|
| Gold | for the sun rays |
| Green | of the pine clad hill supplying wood for the principal industry of pulp and paper manufacture. |
| White | for the winter snows. |
| Imperial red | to denote British origins. |
| Brown | as a symbol of the vast mineral wealth of the Province. |

In 1972, the Minute of Provincial Affairs of the Province petitioned the Lord Lyon to record the tartan in the Writs section of the Lyon Court Books. This was approved on 3 September 1973.

| **R** | G | T | W | T | G | **Y** |
|---|---|---|---|---|---|---|
| 12 | 8 | 28 | 8 | 14 | 60 | 8 |

# NORTH WEST TERRITORIES

*Designer* Hugh Macpherson

*Date* 1969

The North West Territories make up nearly 40% of the land area of Canada. They comprise the mainland of Canada, north of the 60° parallel from the shore of the Hudson Bay to Yukon in the west, together with the islands in Hudson and James Bays and all those which stretch northward into the Arctic. There is a great variation in scenery including lowlands, plateaux and mountain ranges with peaks up to 10,000 feet. The climate is hard with long, bitterly cold winters and short, cool summers, although the MacKenzie valley fares better climatically than elsewhere in the territories. The population is sparse on account of the climate and includes Eskimos (Inuit) and Indians.

The North West Territories owe their tartan to an official Canadian commission, which arranged for one to be designed by Hugh Macpherson of Edinburgh. At the suggestion of the commission, the colours are predominantly white and green. The white represents the snow which covers the North West Territories for six months of the year and the green for the other six months.

| **B** | W | R | bK | G | Y | G | Y | G | **Y** |
|---|---|---|---|---|---|---|---|---|---|
| 6 | 18 | 32 | 4 | 50 | 4 | 4 | 4 | 4 | 8 |

# NOVA SCOTIA

*Designer* Mrs Douglas Murray

*Date* 1953

Nova Scotia is surrounded by sea except for the Chignecto isthmus which links it to New Brunswick. It includes Cape Breton Island (see p. 194). Like Newfoundland, it was visited by John Cabot in 1497. Fishing, farming, and mining are important industries. The forests on the higher and more rugged land provide raw materials for the manufacture of wood pulp and paper.

The Nova Scotia tartan came about almost by accident. In 1953 the sheep-breeders association asked the Handicrafts Division of the Department of Trade and Industry to arrange a display for a farming exhibition. Mrs Douglas Murray, President of the Halifax Weavers Guild designed a woollen panel depicting the history of sheep rearing in the province. It included a shepherd. To avoid controversy concerning the choice of the tartan he was wearing, she designed one of her own. This was to become the Nova Scotia tartan, the colours of which, depicting those of the Nova Scotia flag, have the following significance:

| Blue | for the sea. |
| Light and Dark Green | for the evergreen and deciduous trees of Nova Scotia. |
| White | for the surf. |
| Gold | for the Royal Charter. |
| Red | for the lion rampant on the Nova Scotia arms. |

The colours have an added significance in that the Nova Scotia flag is a counterchange of the Scottish Saltire (blue and white) with the red and gold of the Scottish Royal escutcheon superimposed.

The Nova Scotia tartan was adopted officially by the province under an order of the Lieutenant-Governor-in-Council dated 6 September 1955. It was subsequently to be the first tartan recorded in the Books of the Court of the Lord Lyon.

| **R** | Y | DG | LG | DG | LG | DG | B | **W** |
|---|---|---|---|---|---|---|---|---|
| 2 | 4 | 16 | 8 | 4 | 4 | 4 | 10 | 4 |

# ONTARIO (ENSIGN OF)

*Designer* Rotex Limited

*Date* 1965

Ontario is an irregularly shaped province bordering the United States, with an extended shoreline along the great lakes and the St Lawrence. Its capital is Toronto.

Tartans associated with the Province bear the names Ontario, North Ontario and Ensign of Ontario. Ontario is of complex design, being different in warp and weft. Consequently, it bears little resemblance to the majority of Scottish tartans. The Northern Ontario tartan has a normal reversing sett (G14 Y8 B4 W24 B4 G10 T34). Its six colours are representative of the north; grey for the rocks yielding nickel and iron; white for the snow; blue for the lakes and sky; yellow for the gold mined in the area and for sunshine; red brown for the Indians and green for the forests and fields.

The Ensign of Ontario tartan (as illustrated) is also a reversing tartan and owes its inspiration to the Provincial Coat of Arms which was granted to the province by Royal Warrant of Queen Victoria on 26 May 1868. The yellow is taken from the three golden maple leaves which appear on the green background of the lower shield and the red from the cross of St George on the upper part. The black is from the bear of the crest, and the brown from the supporters on either side of the shield, a moose on the left and a deer on the right.

| DG | bK | R | bK | DT | DG | DT | DG | DT | DG | Y | DG | DT | DG | DT |
|----|----|----|----|----|----|----|----|----|----|----|----|----|----|----|
| 48 | 2 | 10 | 2 | 40 | 8 | 8 | 8 | 42 | 8 | 10 | 48 | 8 | 8 | 8 |

# OTTAWA

*Designer* Mrs Jean Docton

*Date* 1966

Ottawa is the capital of the Canadian confederation and the county town of Carleton County in the province of Ontario. It lies on the Ottawa river and is linked by bridges to Hull, which is in Quebec. Originally called Bytown, after the Englishman George By, its name was changed when it was made the capital of the Dominion of Canada.

On 6 September 1966, the Centennial Committee of the City of Ottawa, commissioned Mrs Jean Docton to design a tartan. Mrs Docton had won awards for her textiles and had taught weaving in Ontario and Quebec. In her design she did not adopt the normal practice in Scotland of reversing the sett from each pivot. Instead she chose to alternate a navy block with an azure block both in the warp and weft. As neither block had a central pivot the result was a rather unusual asymmetric sett. The choice of colours of the Ottawa tartan symbolise:

| | |
|---|---|
| Azure blue | The three rivers of the area, Ottawa, Gatineau and Rideau. |
| Navy blue | The Outaouais tribe of Indians from which Ottawa takes its name, Samuel de Champlain, explorer of the area, and the Royal Engineers who built the 'Rideau Canal'. |
| White | The stands of white pine which contributed to the area at the junction of the three rivers. |
| Red | The capital of Canada. |
| Gold | The great golden elm of old Bytown and the Royal Assent making Ottawa the capital of Canada. |

The design was accepted as the official tartan of Ottawa by order of the Council on 21 November 1966.

*Navy Block*

| R | DY | W | DY | W | DY | DB | DY | DB | DY | DB | DY | W | DY | W | DY |
|---|----|---|----|---|----|----|----|----|----|----|----|---|----|---|----|
| 4 | 24 | 4 | 4  | 4 | 4  | 8  | 4  | 12 | 4  | 8  | 4  | 4 | 4  | 4 | 24 |

*Azure Block*

| W | DY | A  | DY | A  | G | A  | G... |
|---|----|----|----|----|---|----|------|
| 8 | 28 | 16 | 4  | 16 | 4 | 16 | 28   |

Because of the complexity of the design, a truncated version of the navy block is sometimes woven as a symmetrical tartan as below.

| R | DY | W | DY | W | DY | DB | DY | **DB** |
|---|----|---|----|---|----|----|----|--------|
| 4 | 24 | 4 | 4  | 4 | 4  | 8  | 4  | 12     |

# PRINCE EDWARD ISLAND

*Designer* Mrs Jean Reed

*Date* 1964

Prince Edward Island is situated in the Gulf of St Lawrence and is Canada's smallest province. It is separated from the mainland provinces of New Brunswick and Nova Scotia by the Northumberland Strait which is only twenty to thirty miles wide. Frequent ferry services ensure that it is not isolated.

Prince Edward Island has been called the 'Cradle of the Dominion' because it was here that the Fathers of Confederation met in 1864, a date marked one hundred years later by the introduction of the Prince Edward Island tartan.

The forests that once covered the island have been cleared to a large extent and much land is now under pasture and field crops. It is the features of the countryside that are represented in the Prince Edward Island tartan.

> The warmth and glow of the fertile soil,
> The green of field and tree,
> The yellow and brown of Autumn,
> The white of surf or a summer snow,
> Rust, green, yellow and white,
> Yes! That's our Island Tartan.

The Prince Edward Island tartan depicted here has been recognised by the provincial government.

An alternative sett is also encountered (*W*4 bK2 G32 bK24 R24 bK2 *W*4).

| **G** | T | G | T | G | T | C | T | Y | T | C | T | G | T | **W** |
|---|---|---|---|---|---|---|---|---|---|---|---|---|---|---|
| 32 | 2 | 4 | 2 | 4 | 24 | 24 | 2 | 4 | 2 | 24 | 24 | 24 | 2 | 4 |

# QUEBEC

*Designer* Rotex Limited

*Date* 1965

Quebec is an emotive name for both a capital city and a province. The city is the oldest in Canada, being founded by Champlain in 1608. Its name may derive from the Indian word for 'the narrows' (kebec) a reference to its strategic position on the St Lawrence River. It was soon to become the centre of French civilisation and trade in North America. Although captured by James Wolfe in 1759 and formally ceded to Great Britain in 1763 by the Treaty of Paris, it has remained linguistically and culturally predominantly French.

The Plaid de Québec tartan owes its inspiration to the Provincial Coat of Arms which in turn reflects the history of the province. The colours of the tartan are taken from the three horizontal divisions of the shield:

Blue     for the field of the upper division containing three fleur de lys.

Green    for the sprig of maple leaves on the lower division.

Red      for the background of the centre division.

Gold     for the lion rampant in the third division and also for the crown of the crest.

White    for the scroll with the motto 'Je me souviens' (I remember).

The tartan is one of a relatively small number of Canadian asymmetric or non-reversing tartans. Fortunately, it is not too complicated and has earned an accepted place in the tartans of Canada.

| DB | G | DB | Y | bK | R | G | R | DB | W | bK | R . . . |
|----|----|----|----|----|----|----|----|----|----|----|----|
| 50 | 10 | 4 | 4 | 4 | 6 | 40 | 40 | 4 | 4 | 4 | 4 |

# SASKATCHEWAN

*Designer* Mrs F. L. Bastedo

*Date* 1961

Saskatchewan is an inland province with entirely arbitrary boundaries. Formerly part of the North West Territories, it was created a province in 1905. The capital is Regina. It is a predominantly agricultural province.

The colours chosen for the Saskatchewan tartan are described as:

| | |
|---|---|
| Gold | for the golden ripe prairie wheat. |
| Brown | for the summer fallow. |
| Green | for Saskatchewan's forests. |
| Red | for the Saskatchewan lily (lilium philadelphicum). |
| Yellow | for the rapeseed flower and sunflower. |
| White | for the snow. |
| Black | for the oil and coal. |

The official description of the two-block tartan is as follows:

*Gold Block* (large)

| DY | R | DY | **Y** | DY | R | DY |
|---|---|---|---|---|---|---|
| 52 | 4 | 2 | 3 | 2 | 4 | 52 |

The gold block is divided into four smaller blocks by the stripes of Red, Gold, Yellow, Gold and Red running across the length and width of the material.

*Brown/Green Block* (small)

| T | G | bK | **W** | bK | G | T |
|---|---|---|---|---|---|---|
| 21 | 11 | 2 | 4 | 2 | 11 | 21 |

The larger and smaller blocks will alternate across the entire width of the material and will follow the same sequence for the length.

Since each block has a central pivot, yellow and white respectively, the tartan is a normal reversing tartan as the thread count indicates.

| **Y** | DY | R | DY | T | G | bK | **W** |
|---|---|---|---|---|---|---|---|
| 3 | 2 | 4 | 52 | 21 | 11 | 2 | 4 |

The tartan was recorded in the Lyon Court Book on 6 October 1961 upon the application of the Agent General of the Province.

# YUKON

*Designer* Mrs Janet Couture
*Date* 1965

Yukon, a sparsely populated territory of Canada, takes its name from the Yukon River. The North West Territories lie to the east, British Columbia to the south, and Alaska to the west. Since 1963, its capital has been Whitehorse, a centre for mining and fur-trapping. The climate is severe, with long cold winters and short warm summers, illuminated by the midnight sun. It is a land of much beauty reminiscent in places of northern Scotland.

The tartan was designed by Mrs Janet Couture. The preliminary designs were executed in 1965, in readiness for Canada's Centennial year (1967). The tartan was intended both as a tribute to the many Scots settlers in the Yukon and as a symbolic representation of the territory.

The significance of the colours of the sett is:

|  |  |
|---|---|
| Blue | Rivers and sky. |
| Magenta (Red) | Fireweed, the flower of Yukon. |
| Purple | Mountains |
| Yellow | Midnight sun. |
| White | Snow. |
| Green | Forests. |

The narrow yellow lines, which when woven appear broken, also represent the nuggets of gold found in Klondike Creek.

Desirous of registering the tartan with the Lord Lyon in Scotland, Mrs Couture sought the help of the Yukon government. On 10 February 1984, The Hon Beatrice Ann Firth, Minister, the Department of Tourism, Recreation and Culture, petitioned the Lord Lyon King of Arms 'for and on behalf of the people of the said Yukon' to record the Yukon tartan in the Books of the Lyon Court (Writs Section) in the form of a Probative Deed. The petition was granted on the 20 October 1984.

| B | Y | B | Y | B | Y | G | W | R | P | B |
|---|---|---|---|---|---|---|---|---|---|---|
| 20 | 1 | 2 | 1 | 4 | 4 | 4 | 4 | 4 | 4 | 20 |

Samples of the Yukon tartan sent to the Scottish Tartans Society show a somewhat different thread count as below.

| B | Y | B | Y | B | Y | G | W | R | P | |
|---|---|---|---|---|---|---|---|---|---|---|
| 32 | 2 | 2 | 2 | 10 | 8 | 8 | 8 | 8 | 8 | ... |

# AMERICAN TARTAN

*Designer* John C. Cumming

*Date* 1975

The United States has more than ten million citizens who reported in the 1980 census that they were of Scottish descent. This represents 5.34% of those who gave particulars of their lineage but there are probably other US citizens with some Scottish blood of which they are not aware. In addition, many people, not directly of Scottish ancestry, support Scottish societies and enjoy such activities as Scottish country dancing, Highland dancing and Highland games. The traditions of Scotland are such that very many people are extremely proud to be associated with them. At the same time American citizens have a strong loyalty to their own country. It is not surprising, therefore, that a demand grew for a tartan which was simultaneously symbolic of both American and Scottish patriotism.

The idea of an American tartan was first conceived by John C. Cumming, who was born in Forfar, Angus and emigrated to the United States in 1929. He served in the US Army during the Second World War. He is both a Drum Major and Pipe Major and plays for the Zor Shrine Temple (Masonic) Band.

The design represents the colours of the American flag, red, white and blue. The intention of the white lines is to give the impression of the stars representing the American states and the tartan is very distinctive. It was presented in 1976 to the First Lady of the United States, Mrs Betty Ford.

The tartan has an American copyright number GP121829 and the date of publication was 13 August 1975.

| **B** | R | B | W | B | W | B | W | **R** |
|----|----|----|----|----|----|----|----|----|
| 4 | 42 | 2 | 8 | 14 | 4 | 4 | 4 | 4 |

# AMERICAN (ST ANDREWS)

*Designer* Initiated by J.C. Thompson F.S.T.S.
Modified by J.D. Scarlett F.S.T.S.

*Date* 1975

There are differing opinions as to whether the American St Andrews tartan preceded the American tartan, previously described, or vice versa. Mr J.C. Thomson, a fellow of the Scottish Tartans Society, put forward the case for such a tartan in the January 1974 issue of *The Highlander*, the popular American journal on Scottish affairs. 'There is no reason' he wrote, 'why we should not have an identifying tartan for American St Andrews and Caledonian Societies. It could be worn by those who have no other tartan they prefer, or as an alternate sett for any member'. In 1975, the St Andrews Society of Washington DC voted to commission a tartan, initially in connection with the American Bicentennial of 1976. The initial design proposed was the one suggested by J.C. Thompson in *The Highlander,* but when submitted to the Scottish Tartans Society certain changes were suggested by Mr Jim Scarlett, also a fellow of the Scottish Tartans Society. The revised sett, after further slight modifications, was formally adopted with the blessing of the Scottish Tartans Society.

In the final design given here, the dark blue and red are the same colours as the Stars and Stripes and Union Jack. The medium blue and azure are intended to provide an even gradation from the dark blue to the white. Where the lighter stripes cross each other in the dark blue, there is an effect of the stars of the American flag, the thirteen alternate red and white stripes of which appear in a full sett of the tartan.

The American Bicentennial Commission stated policy was that it was not empowered to authorise any design as the sole and official Bicentennial tartan. Nevertheless, the sett below was widely accepted as the American Bicentennial tartan until it became generally known as the American St Andrews. This was the intention of the Washington St Andrews Society, which hoped to see the sett outlive the Bicentennial celebrations. This it has certainly done.

| B | A | W | A | B | bK | R | W | R | W | R | W | R |
|---|---|---|---|---|---|---|---|---|---|---|---|---|
| 28 | 4 | 4 | 4 | 40 | 40 | 34 | 8 | 6 | 6 | 6 | 6 | 10 |

# CAROLINA

*Designer* Micheil MacDonald F.S.T.S.
for the Scottish Tartans Society

*Date* 1981

The states of North Carolina and South Carolina lie to the south of Virginia and border the Atlantic Ocean. In 1629 King Charles I granted Carolana (Carolina) to Sir Robert Heath who did not succeed in founding a colony. The settlement of Carolina was the result of a renewed interest in British overseas expansion after the restoration of the monarchy in 1660. A charter for the colonisation of the region was granted in 1663.

The Cape Fear region was the largest settlement of Highlanders who arrived prior to the American Revolution. Among the immigrants was Flora MacDonald, famous for her rescue of 'Bonnie Prince Charlie'. The Highlanders, most of whom had taken an oath of loyalty to the Crown after the failure of the '45', took up arms against the Americans in 1775. They were defeated and captured in a short battle at Moors Creek Bridge, now a National Military Park. Although a few returned to Scotland or emigrated to Canada, the majority became valued citizens of the new United States.

The mountainous western areas of Carolina are peopled by the descendants of the Scots/Irish migration. The beautiful scenery of the Blue Ridge Mountains nowadays provides the unforgettable setting for one of America's most well-known Scottish events, the Grandfather Mountain Highland Games.

The design of the Carolina tartan is based upon a version of the Royal Stewart tartan taken from a fragment of a coat of the Royal Company of Archers dated c.1730. It is believed to be the same sett as was used for wedding ribbons on the coat of Charles II for his nuptials in 1661. The concept of designing a district tartan to emphasise the link with the Stuart monarch, from whom its name derives, was that of Micheil MacDonald of the Scottish Tartans Society. He put his proposal in 1980 to John Kerr of the St Andrews Society of North Carolina and later to the St Andrews Society of Charleston, South Carolina. The Scottish Tartans Society approved the design in 1981.

| **R** | A | bK | Y | bK | W | bK | R | G | R | bK | R | **W** |
|---|---|---|---|---|---|---|---|---|---|---|---|---|
| 64 | 28 | 32 | 6 | 6 | 8 | 8 | 2 | 56 | 26 | 8 | 8 | 4 |

# DUNEDIN

*Designer* William L. Matthews

*Date* 1986

Dunedin, situated on the water front in Florida, is the first city in the United States to have its name given to a district tartan as a result of a petition to the Scottish Tartans Society by one of its local businesses. The Dunedin district tartan was sponsored by Dunedin Scottish through its proprietor William L. Matthews, who designed it.

At first glance, the Dunedin tartan clearly has a resemblance to the Edinburgh district tartan from which it is derived. Closer examination, however, reveals many subtle differences. Although the colours of each tartan are identical, the transposition, or change, of the shades of the narrower bands of the Edinburgh sett, coupled with the doubling of the green ground and a few minor changes of proportion in other colours, has given the Dunedin tartan a distinct character of its own.

The connection between the two tartans was held by the Council of the Scottish Tartans Society to be acceptable, even desirable, since Dunedin is an anglicized form of the Gaelic name for Edinburgh, Duneideann.

The differences between the setts were such, nevertheless, that the Dunedin tartan could be regarded as a unique and original design. However, there is no reason why the two tartans should not exist side by side. Accordingly, on 9 March 1987, it was granted a Certificate of Accreditation under the seal of the Scottish Tartans Society. Because the Dunedin tartan has been formally accredited by the Scottish Tartans Society, it has found favour with many residents of Dunedin and the surrounding areas.

| **bK** | R | G | C | R | C | bK | B | **W** |
|----|---|----|----|---|---|----|----|---|
| 6 | 6 | 42 | 16 | 6 | 8 | 6 | 52 | 6 |

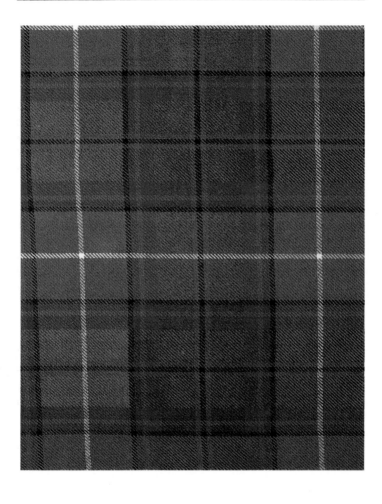

# GEORGIA

*Designer* Peter E. MacDonald F.S.T.S.
for the Scottish Tartans Society

*Date* 1982

The State of Georgia borders the Atlantic to the east, Alabama to the west, the Carolinas and Tennessee to the north and Florida to the south. Georgia was named after the British monarch, George II and was the last of the original states of the American Union to be established as a British colony. On 9 June 1732, King George granted a charter, authorising the new settlement, to James Edward Oglethorpe who landed with an initial group of 114 emigrants on 12 February 1733. The first settlement was made at Savannah. In the early years, General Oglethorpe came to rely on a band of Highlanders from Inverness-shire led by John 'Mohr' MacIntosh. On 2 May 1740, the General ordered Captain MacIntosh, by then commander of the Darien Militia, to form a 'Highland Independent Company of Foot'. This company, in 1746, was reported to be wearing the Government or 'Black Watch' tartan.

The Georgia tartan was designed by the Scottish Tartans Society to commemorate the 250th anniversary of the founding of Georgia and formally presented to the Governor of Georgia in 1982. The granting of the charter by King George is symbolised by red and azure tones taken from a contemporary royal tartan used on a jacket of the Royal Company of Archers (the personal Bodyguard to the Sovereign in Scotland). The forming of the Independent Highland Company of Foot by General Oglethorpe is expressed in the choice of the green field and black over stripes of the government sett worn by the company and the role of the Company Commander, Captain MacIntosh by the underlying elements of the earliest known MacIntosh tartan.

The Georgia tartan has become very popular. It has been adopted as the logo for the cover of the annual programme of the famous Stone Mountain Highland Games held in Atlanta, Georgia's capital.

| G | bK | G | bK | G | bK | A | R |
|----|----|----|----|----|----|----|----|
| 72 | 4 | 4 | 4 | 6 | 24 | 20 | 40 |

# IDAHO (CENTENNIAL)

*Designer* Jan Crook

*Date* 1989

Idaho is one of the inland states of the United States of America. To the north lies Canada, to the east Montana and Wyoming, to the south Utah and Nevada and to the west Oregon and Washington. The State of Idaho was established in 1890 by action of the United States Congress and became the 43rd star in the US flag.

Idaho was explored by early Scots fur traders, and Finan MacDonald along with David Thompson established the first commercial enterprise in the state on 11 September 1809 with the establishment of Kullyspell House on Lake Pend Oreille. Many other Scots emigrated to Idaho in the mid 1800s and established sheep ranches. Boise, the capital, has its own pipe band and an annual Robert Burns Celebration that dates back 70 years. Idaho's ties to Scots heritage are thus well-established and long-standing.

The Idaho Centennial committee has chosen to recognise their important contribution to the state's history by endorsing the Idaho Centennial tartan which was originally promoted by the Kootenai County Centennial Committee.

The Idaho tartan is based on the Black Watch motif and the colours signify the natural features of the State of Idaho:

| | |
|---|---|
| Blue | for the many lakes. |
| Green | for the pine forests. |
| White | for the snow-capped mountains. |
| Tan | for the desert areas and the potato. |
| Garnet | for the native American and the minerals. |

| **B** | R | B | R | B | G | W | T | W | G | B | R | **B** |
|---|---|---|---|---|---|---|---|---|---|---|---|---|
| 24 | 4 | 4 | 4 | 4 | 20 | 24 | 6 | 24 | 20 | 22 | 4 | 4 |

# MAINE

## Maine State Tartan

*Designer:* Sol (Sliomas) Gilis

*Date* 1964

The State of Maine has an international border with Canada and projects northwards between the Canadian Provinces of Quebec and New Brunswick. Much of its scenery resembles the Scottish Highlands, with mountains to the west and wooded islands to the south along the Gulf of Maine. Maine is known as the Pine Tree State and a conifer is included in its state seal.

The Main tartan is certainly the oldest of American State tartans, having been designed in 1964 by Mr Sol (Sliomas) Gilis of Yarmouth, Nova Scotia. Its colours were chosen to suggest the physical characteristics of the State:

Azure Blue for the sky.
Royal Blue for the waters.
Green for the forests
and Red for the bloodline of the people.

The design has always been produced by private businesses, and 'Maine Tartan', 'Maine State Tartan', and 'Tartan of Maine' have served as private trademarks of its manufacturers. It was originally woven in Montreal, with a wide variety of products made in Yarmouth, Nova Scotia, and sold in Maine by 'Tweeds of Maine', a Skowhegan, Maine based corporation. Shortly after 1965, production was stopped.

It is an attractive tartan, and since being rediscovered in 1987, has regained its popularity, and is now being produced by the Maine Tartan and Tweed Company, Inc., of Plymouth, Maine, USA. The tartan is copyrighted in the US Copyright Office under the registration number RE 635,826, and is reproduced here with the kind permission of the copyright owners.

| A | R | G | RB | A | RB | A | RB | A | RB | G |
|---|---|----|----|---|----|---|----|----|----|---|
| 4 | 4 | 66 | 4 | 4 | 12 | 4 | 4 | 46 | 4 | 4 |

# OHIO

*Designer* Merry Jayne McMichael

*Date* 1984

Ohio, one of the eastern states of the USA, is bordered on the north by Lake Erie and by the State of Michigan. Across the eastern border is Pennsylvania, and to the west, Indiana. It takes its name from the river which delineates its southern border, the Ohio, an Indian word which epitomises riverine beauty.

The idea of an Ohio district tartan was conceived by Merry Jayne McMichael Fischbach, one of the trustees and Vice President of the Ohio Scottish Games Inc. Merry Jayne, a native Ohian, was born and raised in Greater Cleveland and is a first generation Scottish American. She discussed her proposal with the Executive President of the Scottish Tartans Society, one of the joint authors of this book, at the Stone Mountain Highland Games in Atlanta, Georgia in October 1982. On 22 May 1983, the Board of Trustees of the Games formally approved the adoption of such a tartan. Then followed an exchange of letters between Merry Jayne and the Research Co-ordinator of the Scottish Tartans Society, as a result of which modifications were made to the original design. After formal adoption of the final design by the Board of Trustees of the Ohio Scottish Games on 18 March 1984, it was registered by the Scottish Tartans Society on 29 March.

The colours of the Ohio tartan were chosen from the insignia of the state. Gold (DY), azure, blue and green were derived from the State Seal and red, white and blue from the State Flag. Red is also the colour of the Red Cardinal, a bird representative of Ohio. The first public display of the Ohio tartan was on the cover of the Ohio Scottish Games Programme in June 1983.

| B | W | R | B | DY | G | A | B | G |
|---|---|---|---|----|---|---|---|---|
| 32 | 12 | 16 | 6 | 2 | 2 | 6 | 2 | 18 |
| 62 | 24 | 32 | 12 | 4 | 4 | 12 | 4 | 19 |

# TEXAS (BLUEBONNET)

*Designer* June MacRoberts

*Date* 1983

Texas has an area larger than any state of the United States, apart from Alaska. It has a long shoreline along the Gulf of Mexico whilst elsewhere there is a wide diversity of physical landscape, which ranges from the low-lying plains of the southeast to the highlands of the western and southwestern borders with New Mexico and Mexico.

The colours of the Texas (Bluebonnet) district tartan owe their selection to the bluebonnet flower, a member of the lupin family, which is widespread in many parts of Texas and is much loved by its inhabitants. The predominant colour is blue, azure when the flowers first open, darkening to mid-blue as they mature. The flower is reminiscent of the shape of a bonnet, hence its name, and a white section of the 'brim' also changes with the passage of time, becoming flecked with wine red. The green of the tartan symbolises the leaves of the plant and yellow the shade which appears on the growing tip of the flower spike.

The Texas (Bluebonnet) tartan was designed by June Mac-Roberts, proprietor of the 'Thistles and Bluebonnets', a store in Salado, Texas. The final design evolved after an exchange of correspondence with the Research Co-ordinator of the Scottish Tartans Society, which in due course issued a Certificate of Accreditation in respect of the Texas (Bluebonnet) tartan in January 1985.

The tartan was adopted as the Sequicentennial Tartan and is now widely accepted as the Texas district tartan.

| G | R | MB | W | R | W | A | W | A | W | Y |
|---|---|----|---|---|---|---|---|---|---|---|
| 16 | 4 | 32 | 4 | 4 | 4 | 32 | 4 | 32 | 4 | 4 |

# TULSA

*Designer* S.C.O.T.

*Date* 1978

Tulsa, the capital of Tulsa County, is situated on the Arkansas River in Oklahoma, a state much settled by Scots.

In 1976, the Scottish Club of Tulsa (S.C.O.T.) under the Presidency of Ed. Morrison, an attorney, conceived the idea of a Tulsa district tartan as a tribute to the City of Tulsa and the founders of S.C.O.T., Mr and Mrs Cecil Shilling. The task of designing a suitable sett was entrusted to a committee, comprising Richard L. Crawford, as Chairman, Chinnubbie McIntosh and Mrs Bea Notley. The project took two years to develop and was supported by the Mayor of Tulsa, Robert J. La Fortune, who on 31 January 1978 issued a proclamation to 'endorse and ordain the establishment' of the Tulsa tartan. The Mayor considered that an official tartan recognised by the Scottish Tartans Society would strengthen ties with the ancestral homeland of thousands of Tulsa citizens. On 19 April 1978, the design was formally approved by the Monitoring Committee of the Scottish Tartans Society.

The Tulsa district tartan is symbolic of the heritage of Oklahoma. Red signified the Native Americans population of the area. Green stands for the Green County of the northeast quadrant of the state. Blue symbolises the lakes and rivers which are important to industry and sportsmen. Black typifies the oil which has played a significant role in Oklahoma's history, society and economy.

| **G** | B | G | R | bK | **R** |
|-------|----|----|----|----|-------|
| 26 | 16 | 26 | 28 | 6 | 28 |

# WASHINGTON

*Designers* Margaret McLeod van Nus
Frank Cannonita

*Date* 1988

Washington State is bordered by Canada to the north and the Pacific Ocean to the west. Its southern boundary with Oregon is marked by the Columbia river and the 46th parallel. To the east lies Idaho. It is a land of spectacular scenery. Near the Pacific coast are the Olympic Mountains and eastwards on the other side of a lowland plain, the Cascade Mountains extend from the Canadian border to the Columbia Gorge. The numerous forests have earned Washington the evocative description of 'The Evergreen State'.

The Washington State tartan was a project of the Vancouver U.S.A. Country Dancers. It was designed in 1988 by Margaret McLeod van Nus and Frank Cannonita in order to commemorate the Washington State Centennial celebrations.

Its colours represent the principal features of the Washington State:

Green:   The background of the rich forests of Washington, the 'Evergreen State'.
Blue:    The blue overlay and stripe: the lakes, rivers and ocean
White:   The snow-capped mountains
Red:     The apple and cherry crops
Yellow:  The wheat and grain crops
Black:   The eruption of Mt St Helens

The Washington State tartan passed through the necessary legislative procedures during 1991. The State Senate approved the legislation adopting the design on February 8th and the House of Representatives on April 8th. Governor Booth Gardner signed the bill into law on May 3rd. The Certificate of Enrollment of Senate Bill 5047 (Chapter 62, Laws of 1991) became effective on July 28th. The Council of the Scottish Tartans Society affixed its seal to the official Certificate of Accreditation on November 8th.

| **Y** | bK | LB | G | A | MR | **W** |
|----|----|----|----|----|----|----|
| 4 | 6 | 6 | 98 | 34 | 8 | 6 |

# DUTCH

*Designer* John Cargill for the Scottish Tartans Society

*Date* 1965

The Netherlands is bounded to the east and south by Germany and to the west and north by the North Sea. It is a constitutional monarchy under the House of Orange. The concept of a Dutch tartan was first put forward by Frank, Theak and Rookilly Ltd., a firm of tie manufacturers in London. There is a good market for tartan ties in Holland partly because many of the residents there are anxious to show publicly their Scottish connections. The Dutch tartan was not intended to take the place of Scottish tartans, but rather as a compliment to those Dutch people who support Scotland. The firm approached the Scottish Tartan Society for assistance.

The late John Cargill, a member of the Society's advisory panel suggested that the Dutch tartan should include that country's national colours and should be based on the sett of the tartan of a Highland Chief who was known to have Dutch connections. In consequence, Lord Reay, Chief of the Mackays, was approached on the matter since his family had had a long association. One of the Society's Patrons, the late Sir Iain Moncrieffe of that Ilk, Albany Herald, gave further advice:

> 'It should be based on Mackay tartan because of the special association of the Clan Mackay and its Chiefs with Holland in general (Baron Aeneas Mackay was Prime Minister of the Netherlands 1889 and his great-grandson Lord Reay, the present Chief, owner of the Kasteel of Ophemert and is also a Dutch baron) and with the Scots-Dutch Brigade in particular (twelve Mackays of Lord Reay's immediate relations were officers in that Brigade between 1673 and 1783 ... General Hugh Mackay, killed at Steinkirk, was one of William III's best commanders). The Mackays were undoubtedly the principal clan in the Dutch context.'

The sett chosen was John Cargill's proposal of a simple colour change in respect of the two tartans, the Dutch and the Dutch Dress. The manner in which these were devised from the Mackay tartan is set out below.

*Mackay*

| bK | G | bK | G | B | G |
|----|----|----|----|----|----|
| 6 | 28 | 28 | 4 | 28 | 6 |

*Dutch*

| bK | O | bK | O | B | W |
|----|----|----|----|----|----|
| 2 | 24 | 24 | 2 | 24 | 4 |

*Dress*

| bK | O | bK | A | W | R |
|----|----|----|----|----|----|
| 2 | 24 | 24 | 2 | 24 | 4 |

**New Brunswick**

| Block 1 | Forest Green | 57 | | |
|---|---|---|---|---|
| | Azure | 2 | | |
| | Gold | 2 | | |
| | Azure | 2 | Stripe 1 | |
| | Gold | 2 | 10 ends | |
| | Azure | 2 | | |
| | Forest Green | 2 | | Black |
| | Meadow Green | 4 | | |
| | Forest Green | 4 | | Black |
| | Meadow Green | 4 | Check 1 | |
| | Forest Green | 4 | 24 ends | Black |
| | Meadow Green | 4 | | |
| | Forest Green | 2 | | Black |

Stripe 2 10 ends as 1
Check 2 24 ends as 1
Stripe 3 10 ends as 1

| | Forest Green | 57 | | |
|---|---|---|---|---|
| | Total | 192 ends | | |

| Block 2 | Red | 18 | | |
|---|---|---|---|---|
| | Beaver Brown | 10 | | |
| | Red | 29 | | |
| | Gold | 4 | | White |
| | Red | 9 | | |
| | Beaver Brown | 32 | | |
| | Red | 21 | | |
| | Azure | 8 | | |
| | Gold | 5 | | |
| | Ship Grey | 3 or 4 | | |
| | Gold | 2 or 1 | | White |
| | Red | 47 | | |
| | Total | 188 | | |
| Block 3 | as Block 1 | | | |
| Block 4 | as Block 2 in reverse | | | |

*Summary*

Block 1  192
Block 2  188
Block 3  192

This sett is very complicated and is generally much simplified when commercially woven.

# Errata and Addenda

p. 13  Para. 1, line 1: "1986" should read "1982"
       Para. 1, line 5: "1682" should read "1732"

p. 22  Last line: "C" should read "G"
              8                    8

p. 32  Para. 4, line 1: "Ian" should read "Iain"

p. 34  Para. 3, line 1: "as" should read "was"

p. 39  The plate illustrates the reversing sett

p. 41  The plate illustrates Wilson's "Caledonia No 45"

p. 44  Para. 1, line 10: "Highlander's" should read "High-
       landman's"

p. 58  The correct threadcount for East Kilbride is

| **W** | R | bK | B | bK | B | bK | G | R | **Y** |
|-------|----|----|----|----|----|----|----|----|-------|
| 8 | 56 | 4 | 20 | 4 | 20 | 4 | 30 | 42 | 8 |

p. 64  Date "c. 1900" should read "c. 1840"
       Para. 2, line 3: "1900" should read "1840"

p. 128  Para. 3, line 3: "General James Grant of Ballin-
        dalloch" should read "Sir James Grant of Grant"

p. 130  Para. 2, line 6: "It is worn" should read "In darker
        colours it is worn"

p. 246  The complete New Brunswick in a traditional revers-
        ing threadcount is as follows:

| **A** | Y | A | DG | LG | DG | LG | DG | LG | DG | A | Y | A | Y | A |
|-------|----|----|----|----|----|----|----|----|----|----|----|----|----|----|
| 2 | 2 | 2 | 2 | 4 | 4 | 4 | 4 | 4 | 2 | 2 | 2 | 2 | 2 | 2 |

| DG | R | T | R | Y | R | T | R | A | Y | N | Y | R | DG | A |
|----|----|----|----|----|----|----|----|----|----|----|----|----|----|----|
| 56 | 18 | 10 | 30 | 4 | 8 | 32 | 20 | 8 | 6 | 4 | 2 | 48 | 56 | 2 |

| Y | A | Y | A | DG | LG | DG | LG | DG | LG | DG | A | Y | **A** |
|----|----|----|----|----|----|----|----|----|----|----|----|----|-------|
| 2 | 2 | 2 | 2 | 2 | 4 | 4 | 4 | 4 | 4 | 2 | 2 | 2 | 2 |

p. 257  Para. 1, line 6: "been granted" should read "applied
        for"

# APPENDICES

## 1 WHICH TARTAN SHOULD I WEAR?

The answer from a strictly legal point of view, is 'any tartan you choose'. Many people choose a tartan skirt, or scarf, because the colours please them. Tartan is fashionable and its widespread popularity is a tribute to its long ancestry. Wearing tartan as a fashion, and wearing it with Highland traditions in mind, are however two entirely different matters. Would-be wearers of tartan, who plan at the same time to associate themselves closely with such traditions, would be well advised to use criteria other than a pleasing appearance when making their choice. Tartans sometimes arouse strong emotions and wearers of what is so quintessentially a means of identification should bear this in mind when attending a Highland function whether it be in the British Isles or overseas. Indeed outwith Scotland itself, especial caution is called for. Many people care little on such occasions what tartan anyone is wearing, but some do and can be vocal about it. Choosing a tartan, therefore, depends to a large extent upon the circumstances in which it is to be worn.

As a feature of fashion, the choice is unlimited since there are no rules other than what is pleasing to the eye. In Highland circles, although no laws exist, custom limits one's choice. It is advisable to choose a tartan which is in some ways associated with one's background. 'Where do my loyalties lie?' is a good question to ask oneself. Loyalties can take many forms, to one's family, to the district where one lives or was born, to one's regiment — to name some of the most important. In choosing a tartan, an obvious possibility is one associated with one's surname.

If that name be the same as that of one of the major 'clans' or 'houses' which have a 'Chief of the Name' recognised by the Lord Lyon, the choice is simplified. Virtually all such families have tartans of their own and some, such as the Gordons, have more than one.

Having a 'clan' surname, however, does not carry an inherent right to wear the appropriate tartan. It is a mistake to ask 'What tartan am I entitled to?' By custom the right to determine the sett and colour of of a clan tartan is vested in the Chief. Custom, however, is a powerful factor in human relationships. To be accepted socially is often a matter of observing local customs with propriety. Many people consider it unethical not to ask the permission of the Chief before wearing a 'clan' tartan. Nowadays, this usually takes the form of joining the appropriate clan association where such exists. One clan chief the Right Hon. the Earl of Lauderdale, has succeeded in ensuring that the Clan Maitland tartan is sold only to persons able to produce specific authorisation from himself.

Having joined a clan association, the new 'clansman' needs to bear in mind that not all tartans sold commercially under a specific name are approved by the Chief concerned. For example, the so called 'Dress Campbell' is not recognised by the present Duke of Argyll, the Chief of the Campbells. It would be a foolish person who wished to be accepted as a member of a clan whilst at the same time disregarding the wishes of the Chief.

'But what if I do not bear the name of a family which has a Chief' the aspiring tartan-wearer may enquire? This, of course, is quite probable since only just over a hundred Scottish families have such a chief. There are millions of Scots throughout the world who have surnames quite different from those borne by the 'Chiefs of the (Whole) Name'. It is with these millions in mind that the following observations are addressed.

Many 'Chiefs of the (Whole) Name' will accept into their clans individuals bearing specific surnames different from their own. These family name groups are loosely called 'septs'. The definition of a 'sept' is a matter which arouses a degree of controversy and for this reason some people prefer to use the terms 'sub', 'dependent' or 'allied' families. A particular surname may be listed as a 'sept' of more than one clan. There is some historical justification for this, since certain surnames are common to more than one 'Clan territory'. To overcome this problem, the potential clansman might wish to ascertain with which area his forefathers were associated and choose accordingly. Septsmen usually wear the tartan of the clan to which they belong. Some 'sept' names, however, have a specific tartan of their own.

The Lord Lyon has authority from the Crown to grant 'territorial designations' to certain landowners in which the name of the estate becomes an integral part of that person's name, for example, Teall of Teallach. Some of these estates may be of considerable antiquity, being feudal baronies or superiorities.

When an estate has been in the same family for more than three generations, and bears the same name as its owner, the designation is often '——— of that ilk'. Indeed, it is possible for such a designation to remain, even though the lands to which it originally related have been sold.

Many heads of territorial houses have a tartan of their own and are sometimes willing to give permission for this to be worn by persons bearing the same surname, even though they are not in the direct line of descent.

Not all Heads of Territorial Houses have pledged loyalty to a 'Chief of the (Whole) Name' but whenever they have done so their House becomes a 'House within a House' on such terms as mutually agreed.

Other 'sept' names may be the same as those of someone to whom a grant of arms has been made by the Lord Lyon but who has no territorial designation. A number of armigers in this category also have a tartan of their own and they too may be willing for this to be worn by others of the same name, but this should never be done without permission.

Some names, recognised by the Lord Lyon as 'organised Scottish families', do not have a Chief, because the requirements laid down by the Lyon Court with regard to a 'Chief of the Name' have not been met, or because no individual has succeeded in establishing a claim to preside over others of the same name. Such chiefless 'clans' nevertheless have tartans of their own.

To the aspiring wearers of tartan, the search for setts associated with their name may prove to be to no avail. Fortunately, however, they still have a very wide choice. For a few, there are the corporate tartans accredited by the Scottish Tartans Society. Modern companies have certain attributes which are reminiscent of the clans of yesteryear, in particular loyalty to a common ideal and the working together for the common good. As a means of identification, corporate tartans share much in common with today's clan associations and are often proudly worn by employees of the company.

For the majority, however, the choice of a corporate tartan is not available. For subjects of H.M. the Queen, the Hunting Stewart has been an accepted 'universal tartan' and for professed Jacobites 'The Jacobite' tartan is a possibility. The Lord Lyon Court Office has suggested the 'Government' tartan (in its regimental form) as a universal tartan, but because of its other associations, this is not always a popular choice.

It is to the district tartans that people outwith clans now look. As can be seen in this book, there are more than one hundred to choose from. There can scarcely be anybody who loves Highland traditions that cannot find a tartan associated with their own life or that of one of their forefathers. For those who seek a community identity as well, many organisations welcome the wearers of district tartans, to name but two, the Scottish Tartans Society and the District Families Association (U.S.A.).

Many who choose to wear district tartans do so as an alternative to their clan or other usually-worn sett. Some may even wish to identify themselves with more than one district. Those wishing to wear district tartans should be aware of some of the customs that are associated with their use as part of Highland dress. There are no rules or regulations as such, other than tradition and good taste.

It is quite permissible for more than one tartan to be worn at the same time. Early portraiture in Scotland gives many examples of this. In day wear, for example, the kilt could be in the district tartan and the plaid in the clan or family tartan or vice versa. Good taste demands, however, that there is some harmony of colour between the two setts. Generally, it is not advisable to mix ancient colours in the one tartan with modern colours in the other, though ancient colours in some setts blend quite well with reproduction colours in another. It is all a matter of aesthetics.

It is not general practice to wear different tartans in formal evening dress, but it is a matter of personal preference. Usually, because they are smaller in size than day plaids, the shoulder plaids worn for evening wear look better if they match the kilt.

If a district tartan is worn as the sole tartan, it is usual to replace the clansman badge crest with a more general badge, such as a thistle. This would not necessarily apply to an armiger. In Scotland, in a few cases, there are official crests granted by the Lord Lyon, appertaining to the local government district council, which gives its name to a particular tartan (e.g. East Kilbride). This could be worn as a cap badge in the form of a clan crest badge, if the authority gave permission.

In selecting a tartan, the would-be wearer has nowadays a very wide choice. One needs only to be guided by common sense, applied with respect and courtesy for the opinions and feelings of others. Remember, there are no rules other than custom.

# 2  THE LAW OF SCOTLAND CONCERNING TARTANS

Tartans cannot be exactly compared to armorial bearings, which if matriculated by the Lord Lyon, are protected by the Law of Scotland and cannot legally be used without the consent of the person to whom they were granted. Indeed, in Scotland, the unauthorised use of armorial bearings could lead to a fine or even imprisonment.

Tartans, on the other hand, carry no legal protection, unless they be modern setts registered as 'Trade Designs' under the United Kingdom of Great Britain and Northern Ireland and Isle of Man Registered Designs Act, 1949. Samples of the tartan to be registered have to be lodged at the Design Registry in London. Copyright in the Design lasts for five years from the date of registration, and may be extended for two further periods, each of five years. After this maximum of fifteen years, the design may be woven by anybody without restriction. A registered design of this nature, however, only gives the proprietor the exclusive right to control the weaving of the registered tartan. It is questionable whether the law could be evoked to prevent anybody wearing such a tartan. Similar provisions may apply in other countries outwith the jurisdiction of this act.

The majority of tartans, have been in existence far too long to be eligible for registration with the Design Registry or corresponding overseas institutions. The sett of most tartans, therefore, is a matter of tradition rather than of legal exclusivity. The inclusion of a tartan in the Register of All Publicly Known Tartans of the Scottish Tartans Society, or in the specialised records of the Lyon Court, does not of itself confer any proprietary right enforceable under the law of Scotland. The Register of All Publicly Known Tartans of the Scottish Tartans Society, and the records of the Lyon Court might, nevertheless, be regarded by a Court of Law in the United Kingdom as evidence in cases brought under the Trades Description Act of 1968 if an incorrectly named tartan were to be marketed.

It has been suggested recently by a copyright lawyer that in the United Kingdom newly designed tartans are protected under the new copyright law (1988). If this is so, the protection of an original design would be extended to fifty years. Whether an unauthorised copying of an original tartan design is an infringement of copyright is an issue which only a court of law could decide. As yet, no such determination has been made in the United Kingdom. A proposal has been made that The Scottish Tartans Society should bring forward a collective action in the courts on behalf of tartan designers to settle the matter once and for all. If successful, designers would be able to prevent the unauthorised use of their designs, or to demand a royalty.

Manufacturers proposing to weave newly introduced tartans should enquire whether or not the design is registered at the Design Registry in the United Kingdom, or similar institution overseas. If it is, then permission will be required from the holder of the registered design. In such cases, it is usual to pay either a royalty or a commission on the total sales. Even if the design is not so entered at the Design Registry, manufacturers and retailers of new tartans might care to bear in mind that it costs quite a lot of money to develop a tartan. The more responsible members of the trade already pay a royalty on the weaving of new tartans either to the organisation which initiated the design, or when requested to do so by that organisation, to the Scottish Tartans Society, which maintains the Register of All Publicly Known Tartans. It is to be hoped that this practice may be extended.

# 3  THE COURT OF THE LORD LYON WITH REGARD TO TARTANS

A great deal of confusion arises concerning the precise role fulfilled by the Lord Lyon King of Arms, with regard to tartans. Statements such as '... the Lord Lyon's office ... controls the use of authentic Scottish tartans' appear from time to time in even well-regarded journals.[1] Such misleading comments arise from partial knowledge or misunderstanding of the true position.

The Court of the Lord Lyon is primarily an office of heraldic jurisdiction.[2] Tartans, per se, are not heraldic devices, although they can become so if incorporated in armorial bearings. One suspects the hand of Sir Thomas Innes of Learney, late Lord Lyon, in the following observation:

> 'During the past few years, ..., whenever a person or limb attired in 'the proper tartan of clan X ...' occurs in armorial bearings, Lyon Court takes evidence, and defines such tartan, the system of definition adopted being ... the Logan system of one eighth inch proportions ... A record of authentic clan tartans is thus being gradually built up on legal evidence and statutory authority, in the Public Register of All Arms and Bearings in Scotland, one of the National Public Registers of the kingdom.'[3]

This statement, though true in itself, is possibly the source of many presentday misconceptions. It is perhaps not generally realised that relatively few heraldic achievements depict tartan. Indeed, only twenty-eight tartans are defined in the Public Register of All Arms and Bearings in Scotland, whilst a further two are mentioned but not defined. Nevertheless, it is the custom of Scotland to regard the use of a clan or family tartan as being the heritable prerogative of the respective Chief or head. Though this prerogative is not enshrined in the law of Scotland, the customary privileges of Chiefs relating to clan tartans are recognised by the Lord Lyon.

It is also the prerogative of the Lord Lyon to record upon application the thread count of a tartan in the Lyon Court Books. This book is used also for placing upon public record such matters as Change of

Name when this is authorised by the Lyon Court. Precisely which tartans are recorded in the Lyon Court Book is entirely a matter of discretion for the Lord Lyon. Accordingly, therefore, since the practice was initiated in 1951, the criteria has varied according to the views of the incumbent of the office. The Lord Lyon seeks technical advice with regard to the inclusion of tartans in the Public Register of all Arms and Bearings in Scotland and in the Lyon Court Book from his Tartan Committee which comprises individuals having a specialised knowledge on tartans. There is often a need for this Committee to liase with the Scottish Tartans Society and indeed particular individuals may well be members of both bodies.

Between 1951 and 1992, thirty-nine separate entries were made in the Lyon Court Book in respect of the thread counts of specific tartans. Two of these entries also included a hunting tartan and two a dress tartan, bringing the total of tartans so recorded to forty-three. Of these thirty-three were applicable to personal surnames, and nine to Provinces of Canada and one to the United States Military Academy at West Point, New York. Apart from Nova Scotia, the arms for which have been matriculated by the Lyon Court, the registration of the tartans of the remaining provinces and the West Point Military Academy has been a matter of some controversy. The present Lord Lyon, Sir Malcolm Innes of Edingight, who succeeded to his office in 1981, has stated that with regard to tartans, he will 'only consider Petitions from Chiefs of the Name as they are the only people who can determine clan or family tartans. In certain exceptional cases, where a significant local authority or government authority have by legislation determined a tartan' he will also consider a Petition from them either before a tartan has been determined by such legislation or after. He is not prepared to 'accept Petitions from individuals for tartans'[4] and has suspended the former practice of recording tartans of those with matriculated arms who are not also Chiefs of the Name. Many of those who have considered the matter in depth hold the view that the Lord Lyon should not have become involved with the recording of tartans other than those appertaining to individuals or corporate bodies possessing arms matriculated by the Lyon Court. They reason that it is difficult to understand the constitutional grounds for the Lord Lyon recording tartans of public authorities outwith Scotland other than Nova Scotia, which has arms granted by the Lyon Court. In respect of armorial bearings the Canadian provinces, for example, were formerly under the jurisdiction of the Earl Marshal and Garter King of Arms in London, though they are now the responsibility of the Chief Herald of Canada. Unlike Canada, however, the United States has no connection with the British Crown, of which the Lord Lyon is a judicial officer. Presumably, the assumption was made at the time that tartans are quintessentially Scottish and this in itself was justification (see p. 261).

There is considerable harmony of ideas between the Lyon Court and the Scottish Tartans Society with regard to tartan. There is a historical reason for this. In 1966, the late Lord Lyon, Sir Thomas Innes of Learney detailed to one of the authors of this work, Dr Gordon Teall of Teallach his hopes for the future of the Scottish Tartans Society which he had inaugurated three years previously. These were conveyed to the late Captain Stuart Davidson and in turn to the Administrative Committee of the Society. As it exists today, the Society conforms to those early hopes, due to the continuing voluntary efforts of its members and the dedication of its staff.

### Notes

1   *Let's Go* The inflight magazine of British Caledonian Airways, September/October 1985, p.9.
2   See Information Leaflet No 5 The Court of Lord Lyon.
3   *The Clans, Septs and Regiments of the Scottish Highlands,* by Frank Adams. First published 1908. Revised by Sir Thomas Innes of Learney, 1964. Eighth edition 1970 pp 392, 394.
4   Letter dated 18.1.85

# 4   THE SCOTTISH TARTANS SOCIETY

The Scottish Tartans Society is widely regarded as the principal authority on tartans and Highland dress in the world. Since the convening of its founding members by the late Captain T. S. Davidson and its formal inauguration by the late Lord Lyon, Sir Thomas Innes of Learney, in 1963, the Society has received the support of the majority of those individuals who have devoted their energies to the study of this popular and emotive aspect of Scotland's heritage. Its headquarters occupy the historic premises of the Highland Heritage Museum Trust in Pitlochry, Perthshire, a town known as the 'Heart of the Highlands'.

The Society is in Scottish law a 'recognised charity', that is a non-profit-making organisation. It has been granted the status of an 'Incorporation Noble in the Noblesse of Scotland' by the Lord Lyon King of Arms. It is governed by an elected council which includes representatives of major Scottish institutions and of the local government authorities of the area in which its headquarters are situated.

Membership of the Scottish Tartans Society is open to individuals and corporate institutions which are desirous of supporting its aims and objects. Corporate institutions in membership of the Society include public and private commercial companies, professional bodies, clan associations and other societies.

The Society is required by its constitution, inter alia 'to study the origins, history and development of tartans and to record these in a register of All Publicly Known Tartans. The maintenance of this Register is the most important aspect of the Society's work. It provides the most comprehensive index of tartans in existence and is constantly being updated. The register, which attracts enquiries from all over the world, is described more fully in the following chapter. It has been compiled from the unique archives of the Society. These include a collection of several thousand tartan specimens, some of which date back to the eighteenth century. In addition, the Society has built up a collection of original documents relating to the manufacture, design and use of tartan. This is being steadily added to as more historical material comes to light. To supplement these extensive archives, and in order to assist researchers, the Society had established a library of published works relating directly and indirectly to tartans and Highland dress.

Original research into these subjects is much encouraged by the Society. Fellowship of the Society (F.S.T.S.) may be bestowed upon members who have made an outstanding contribution to research work, although the honour is such that there can be no more than twenty-five individuals in the 'Leet of Fellows' at any one time. Another prestigious honour awarded by the Society's Council is that of 'Heritage Fellow of the Scottish Tartans Society'. This award may be made to any person, not necessarily a member of the Society, who has made a major contribution to fulfilling one of the principal objects of the Society, namely the preservation and appreciation of Scotland's unique cultural heritage. A further award, the 'Scottish Tartans Society's Commendation' is made to members of the Society who have made an outstanding contribution to its success.

At the Annual Conference the Scottish Tartans Society organizes lectures and discussions relating to its field of study. Topics have included, for example: King George IV's visit to Edinburgh in 1822, The Art and Practice of Spinning, Tartans of Clan Campbell, Manx Tartans, the Battle of Sheriffmuir, The Sobieski Stuarts (fraud or fact), District Tartans, etc.

Members of the Society attend Highland gatherings whenever possible giving out information on tartans and Highland dress and answering queries. To supplement these activities, and to satisfy an increasing demand, educational information packs have been produced for school use. The many enquiries received from young people are indicative of the value of the Society's work to the general public.

The Society's contribution to disseminating knowledge about Scotland's heritage is not confined to Scotland alone. Overseas exhibitions are organised from time to time and have taken place, for example in the Isle of Man, Sweden, Japan, Australia and the United States. In the United States, members of the Society meet together at various venues. Representatives provide an Information Service at many Highland Gatherings held in the USA and there is an annual convention during the Stone Mountain Highland Games in Atlanta. At Highlands, North Carolina there is an attractive museum with its own Board of Trustees. Here artefacts from the museum in Scotland are exhibited on a rota basis, allowing for very similar displays to those at Comrie to be on view.

The day-to-day work of the Scottish Tartans Society is financed by membership subscriptions and research fees supplemented by the generosity of benefactors, both private and commercial. The Scottish Tartans Society continues, as required by its constitution, to 'promote the preservation and appreciation of Scotland's unique heritage' and 'to maintain a liaison with other institutions and organisations sharing similar ideals'.

Nothing perhaps summarises the work of the Society more concisely than its armorial bearings granted in 1976 by the Lord Lyon King of Arms. These depict the Saltire of Scotland, the woven threads of tartan, and the tenterhooks upon which the plaids of yesteryear were hung to 'weather'. The aims of the Society are summarised in the motto suggested for it by the late Sir Iain Moncrieffe of that Ilk:

'Bring Forrit the Tartan'.[1]

### Note

1    In November 1857 during the Indian Mutiny, General Sir Colin Campbell was in command of the force responsible for the relief of Lucknow. In the assault on Secundrabagh, in which stood a tall building held by the mutineers, troops of the 4th Punjab Regt. were repeatedly forced back whilst attempting to storm a narrow breach made by artillery fire in the walls. In desperation, Sir Colin turned to Col. Ewart, commanding the old 93rd Regt. the Sutherland Highlanders, who were the 'Thin Red Line' at Balaclava and roared — 'Bring forrit the Tartan ... let my ain lads at 'em!'
Pipe Major John McLeod quickly responded to the General's order by striking up with 'On 'Wi the Tartan' (The Haughs o' Cromdale), and led the Highlanders through the breach in the walls. After fighting hand to hand with 2000 Sepoys for more than four hours, they finally won the day, earning in so doing six Victoria Crosses for bravery of the highest order.

# 5 THE SCOTTISH TARTANS MUSEUM TRUST

Closely associated with the Scottish Tartans Society is the Scottish Tartans Museum Trust, an incorporated charitable company limited by guarantee. This trust is governed by an Executive Board, a majority of the members of which are nominated by the Scottish Tartans Society. The Trust administers the Tartans Museum at Comrie, Perthshire. This has been granted the official status of a Registered Museum and works in close cooperation with the Scottish Museums Council. The museum has a fine collection of men's, women's and children's clothing, dating from the eighteenth century, together with the appropriate accoutrements such as the sgian dubh, dirk, kilt pin, brooch, sporran, etc. Some of these artefacts are of considerable national importance, such as the Duke of Sussex's collection which dates from the early nineteenth century. The Duke of Sussex (1773-1843) was a son of George III. He also bore the title of the Earl of Inverness and in 1815 commissioned a specially designed tartan which was used to make one of the kilts and plaids in the collection. This has come to be known as the Earl of Inverness tartan and is now used as the district tartan of the burgh and county of Inverness (see p. 86).

The museum possesses a number of original paintings, drawings and photographs depicting tartan clad figures, and various items of bric-à-brac such as specimens of Mauchline ware decorated with a tartan design. In the museum, several hundred specimens of woven fabrics illustrating the classes of tartan included in the Register of All Publicly Known Tartans are displayed for visitors to study.

The development of Highland dress through the centuries is illustrated by examples of period costumes from the Society's valuable collection. Other exhibits include, for example, documents from the Society's archives such as letters and invoices from the famous, but now defunct, firm of weavers, Wm. Wilson & Sons of Bannockburn, who were active in the late eighteenth and nineteenth centuries; an original portrait of Queen Victoria's manservant, John Brown in kilt, waistcoat and jacket; drawings and etchings depicting figures in Highland dress, some of well-known personalities such as John Sobieski Stuart, the author of the contentious book on tartans, the *Vestarium Scoticum,* published in 1842, and even Kaiser Wilheim II, Queen Victoria's grandson.

The Museum also contains other curiosities which emphasise the emotional appeal of the tartan, for example a piece of MacBean tartan taken to the moon and back, a distance of 480,000 miles, by Astronaut Alan L. Bean and a crash helmet decorated with Colquohoun tartan and worn by Lady Arran, the racing driver; photographs of the kilted Magi in the Lauderdale Chapel at Haddington recently presented by the Earl of Lauderdale, Chief of the Maitlands.

The Museum, however, is not merely a place for housing static exhibitions of the many aspects of research undertaken by the Scottish Tartans Society into matters relating to tartans and Highland dress. It is also a working Museum in that the weaving of tartan on a hand loom is demonstrated from time to time, as is the use of the spinning wheel. These activities take place at the rear of the Museum in a reconstructed Highland bothy, thatched with heather, and built of stones smoothed and rounded by the glaciers that covered the Comrie area during the ice age.

The garden beyond the bothy contains a collection of plants such as berberis, silver birch, rhubarb, dock and nettle which were used in the past for the manufacture of the natural dyes that provided most of the colours in hand-woven tartans. Occasionally an old iron cauldron may be found boiling as Members of the Scottish Tartans Society, interested in preparing dyes, prove that the ancient art has not been lost.

Under the guidance of Scottish Museum's Council the Tartans Museum has an on-going policy of acquisitions and disposals. Its acquisitions fund is supported by donations from all over the world.

# 6   THE REGISTER OF ALL PUBLICLY KNOWN TARTANS

The Register of All Publicly Known Tartans, maintained by the Scottish Tartans Society, is housed in the Hall of Records of the Highland Heritage Museum Trust at Pitlochry, Perthshire. It records the proportions (thread counts) and colours of more than 2,000 setts. These include not only tartans associated with family names, but also national and district tartans, regimental and other military tartans, society and company tartans, commemorative tartans, named fashion trade setts and the occasional novelty tartan. The Register is constantly being up-dated and provides the most comprehensive record of tartans in the world. It is in constant use: to identify samples; to help people choose a tartan appropriate to their name; to refute false claims of originality. It has been used to help clan chiefs resolve controversies concerning their tartans, to advise the Lord Lyon and to settle trade disputes. In 1992 the Register was computerised in conjunction with the University of Stirling.

The Scottish Tartans Society issues three forms of certificate in relation to the register at the appropriate fees; the basic copy of entry; the full copy of entry; the Council's illuminated Certificate of Accreditation. The basic copy of entry certifies that the tartan is included in the register but gives no other details. The full copy of entry gives the thread count (except for currently registered designs) and the sources and dates when the tartan was first noted. The Society reserves the right, however, to limit the number of certificates issues to any one individual. Information given on such certificates must not be used in publications without the permission of the Scottish Tartans Society. The basic and full copies of entry are purely a matter of record and do not imply that the tartan in question has the approval of a clan chief, 'district' authority or the Council of the Scottish Tartans Society.

The Council's Certificate of Accreditation, however, is an accolade awarded only in respect of tartans which have been formally placed before the Council for formal accreditation by the Scottish Tartans Society. Before Accreditation is granted, the Register of All Publicly Known Tartans is searched to ensure that the tartan in question is original and unlikely to be confused with an existing tartan. Tartans bearing a clan name are not acceptable for this category of the Register without the approval of the Chief of the clan concerned. The Council's Certificate of Accreditation is then issued, under the Council's seal, giving all relevant details of the tartan.

The Society in appropriate cases undertakes the design of new tartans. This service involves discussions with the applicant concerning possible designs, the searching of the Register to ensure that the proposed design is original, the preparation of initial sketches and woven samples, and advice on ordering bolts of cloth. For an additional fee, an original design can be registered with the Design Registry in the United Kingdom which gives the applicant full legal control of the design in that country for a maximum of fifteen years (see p. 251). Enquiries concerning the design or registration of new tartans should be addressed to: The Registrar of Tartans, Register of All Publicly Known Tartans, The Scottish Tartans Society, Pitlochry, Perthshire PH16 5ND.

# 6  GLOSSARY

**ancient**   a term used to describe colours which simulate natural dyes shades in use prior to the mid-eighteenth century. It does not indicate the age of the tartan or sett.

**asymmetrical**   a tartan in which the sett does not reverse itself at regular intervals. The majority of tartan patterns reverse:   left to right, right to left, and again left to right, etc. Asymmetrical setts are read like lines of print, left to right, then beginning at the left again.

**count**   an enumeration of the number of threads in each colour stripe.

**ends**   the thread ends in each colour stripe. The minimum number in each stripe is two.

**ground**   the dominant colour field upon which other colour stripes appear to be superimposed. Although this is usually a solid broad area, due to the perception of colour by the human eye, the ground may not be the largest amount of colour in the pattern.

**guard lines**   narrow lines placed on each side of a wider line to add accent and definition.

**half-wide**   tartan woven in twenty-eight inch width, the maximum which can be woven by hand or on small power looms. Specialty tartans are often woven 'half-wide' while large quantities are fifty-eight inches, full-width.

**modern**   colour shades produced by chemical dyes after the 1860s.

**(whole) name**   a chief of the whole name is a man or woman recognised by the Lord Lyon as being the chief of all persons bearing a particular surname.

**old**   a term used to describe a pattern historically older than the sett in common use.

**pivot**   a central colour stripe used to mark the place where the sett begins to repeat itself backwards. There are two pivots in symmetrical setts.

**reed**   the comb-like part of a loom used to space the warp threads evenly. The number used depends on the size and complexity of the sett.

**repeat**   one reversal of the pattern, left to right and right to left. The complete unit gives a measure of the size of the pattern. The weaver must plan for and centre the number of repeats to be shown on the full web of cloth.

**reproduction**   colours intended to simulate fading or other changes in tartan dyes long exposed to the effects of sun and weather.

**selvedge**   a narrow border on the edge of woven cloth done in a larger thread or different style of weave to prevent unravelling.

**sett**   the pattern of a tartan, once expressed as a description of the width of the colour stripes in fractions of an inch. The convention now is to record the sett by counting the number of threads in each colour stripe from pivot to pivot.

**twill**   a style of weaving where each thread goes over two and under two threads cross-wise to it. All tartan is traditionally woven in twill weave, except at the selvedge.

**warp**   the length-wise threads on the loom. These are pre-strung by the weaver.

**web**   the finished cloth still on the loom.

**weft**   the cross-wise threads. In tartan the sett of the warp and weft are traditionally identical.

## Addendum

**Vancouver Centennial** was recorded by the Lord Lyon on 30th August 1991. This tartan had been in the pipeline since before 4th June 1988, when the Chief Herald of Canada took up his position.

| **R** | B | W | G | Y | **G** |
|-------|-----|-----|-----|-----|-------|
| 2 | 52 | 24 | 48 | 4 | 8 |

# INDEX

Ancient colours, 2
Anderson, Louis, 204
Anderson, W., 26
Arbroath, Oath of, 24
Argyll & Sutherland Regiment, 130
Armstrong Evans, Ms Abi, 140, 144
Baker, Mrs Edyth, 196
Bastedo, Mrs F.L., 218
Black Watch, 32, 130
Bottomley, A.A., 120
Bruce, Lord, 188
Campbell of Cawdor, 28
Canada, tartans for, 184-221
Cargill, John, 244
Clan surnames, 248
Colour, abbreviations, 19
Cornwall, tartans for, 10, 138-45
Couture, Janet, 220
Crook, Jan, 232
Cumming, John C., 222
Dalgleish, D.C., 2, 36
Docton, Mrs Jean, 212
Drennan, Allan C., 112
England, tartans for, 12, 136-55
Fraser, Ross & Co., 66
Galt, Arthur, 42, 110
Gilis, Sol, 234
Gordon, Frank, 48
Grant, Alexander, 8
Grant, Mrs Elizabeth, 194
Grant, James H., 8
Grant, Sir James, 9, 128
Hamilton, Captain, 7
Hannay, John, Councillor, 42, 72
Hastie, J. MacGregor, 52, 104
Highland Society of London, 38
Ireland, tartans for, 11, 168-73
Johnson, W. & A.K., 24, 28, 98, 116
Kelly, C. Ewan, 164
Kinloch Anderson, 52
Lamb, Mrs A., 184
Lawson, G., 108
Loomcrofters, 198, 202
Lyon Court, 248
MacDonald, Micheil, 226
MacDonald, Peter E., 230
MacNaughton's of Pitlochry, 30
Macpherson, Hugh, 60, 206
MacRoberts, June, 236
Macarthur, Peter, 182
Man, Isle of, 10, 156-67

Martin, Martin, 6
Matthews, William L., 228
McMichael, Merry Jayne, 234
McQuaid, Patricia, 156
Modern colours, 2
Moncrieffe, Sir Iain, 244
Moore, T. Richard, 158
Morton-Nance, E.E., 138
Murray, Mrs Douglas, 208
Neilsen, Mrs E., 184
Netherlands, tartan for, 244
Newnham, Gerry, 52
Norse, invasion, 88
Proscription, Act of, 1
Rankine, Hugh K., 200
Rawe, Donald, 140, 144
Redwood, Sandra A., 142
Rees, Gordon, 180
Registry of tartans, 255
Reid, John, 178
Reproduction colours, 2
Richards, D.M., 174
Robertson, Struan, 9
Rotex, Ltd., 210, 216
Royal tartans, 14-15
Samuels, Sidney, 88
Scarlett, James D., 224
Scottish Tartans, 22-133
Scottish Tartans Society, 12, 13, 226, 254
Setts, 17
Sheard, Roy, 146, 148, 152
Smith, Philip D., 34, 118
Stewart of Garth, 5
Stewart, D.C., 46, 52, 84
Stewart, D.W., 46, 62
Tartan, law concerning, 251
Teall of Teallach, Gordon, 58, 156, 164
Thompson, J.C., 224
Thompson, Mrs P.J., 96
Titles of nobility, 14
United States, tartans for, 222-43
Ward, Eric K., 186
Wearing tartan, 247
Weaving, vocabulary, 259
Weiser, David, 192
Wilkinson, Alison, 136
Wilsons of Bannockburn, 5, 22, 28, 40,
   44, 52, 56, 68, 70, 74, 76, 78, 106, 114,
   122, 132, 150
Wood, Robert, 160, 162, 166
Wynes, Fenton, 50